NE 642 .H7 H5 1972

Hind, Arthur Mayger, 1880–
1957.

Wenceslaus Hollar and his
views of London and Windsor

W9-ADE-151

20

DATE DUE

JUL - 5 2005	ALA (Cromwell)	

Demco, Inc. 38-293

WENCESLAUS HOLLAR

WENCESLAUS HOLLAR

Gentilhomme ne a Prage l'an 1607. a esté de nature fort inclin pr l'art de meniature principa-
lemont pour esclaircir, mais beaucoup retardé par son pere, l'an 1627, il est party de Prage aijant
demeure en divers lieux en Allemaigne, il s'est addonne pour peu de temps a esclaircir et apliequer
l'eau forte, estant party de Coloigne avec le Comte d'Arondel vers Vienne et d'illec par Prage
vers l'Angleterre, ou aijant esté serviteur domesticque du Duc de Iorck, il s'est retire de la a cause
de la guerre a Anvers ou il reside encores.

Ie. Meyssens pinxit et excudit.

WENCESLAUS HOLLAR

AND HIS VIEWS OF LONDON
AND WINDSOR
IN THE SEVENTEENTH CENTURY

BY

ARTHUR M. HIND

OF THE BRITISH MUSEUM
SLADE PROFESSOR OF FINE ART IN THE UNIVERSITY OF OXFORD

WITH FRONTISPIECE AND NINETY-SIX ILLUSTRATIONS

BENJAMIN BLOM, INC.
Publishers New York 1972

TO

MY WIFE

First published London, 1922
Reissued 1972 by
Benjamin Blom, Inc.
New York, N.Y. 10025

Library of Congress
Catalog Card Number 68-56500

Printed in the
United States of America

108566

PREFACE

I MAY say at once that I have not set out to write a book on topography. My aim is to present Hollar as an etcher, and to focus interest on him by selecting for illustration a special, and to Englishmen the most attractive, section of his voluminous work. To a general survey of his life and work I have appended a detailed catalogue of all his etched views of London and Windsor, including subject and portrait etchings which contain London backgrounds, thus offering a contribution towards the much greater task of a complete revision of Parthey's catalogue of 1853.

The description of Hollar's etching of the *Tower of London with the Execution of the Earl of Strafford* (No. 23 in my catalogue) as a " contemporary Dutch print " in Besant's *London in the Time of the Stuarts* (1903, p. 39) is one instance among many to show that Hollar is by no means accurately known even by connoisseurs of London archæology, and I hope that my catalogue will serve to clarify one of the chief sources of the study of London topography in the seventeenth century.

I have not ventured on any general account of old London but have added in my catalogue a considerable number of topographical notes relating both to general plans and to buildings on which information is less readily accessible. I claim no originality in topographical research, though in the case of some of the plans I have spent considerable time in sifting evidence, which has led me in some cases to independent conclusions. I have referred freely to the publication of the London Topographical Society, and to Mr. H. B. Wheatley's standard work of reference, *London, Past and Present*. My special thanks are due to Mr. Philip Norman for kind help on sundry questions of topography, and to the Hon. John Fortescue in relation to the incomparable collection of Hollar's etchings under his charge in the Royal Library at Windsor Castle.

I am appending to this preface a reproduction of the postscript to George Vertue's *Description of the Works of Hollar*

(1759), with Vertue's design for a mural tablet to the artist's memory.   Would it not be a graceful act of friendship to the newly-founded Czechoslovak State, as well as a token, long overdue, of the debt Londoners owe to Hollar, if some simple monument of this kind were put up in St. Margaret's, Westminster?

A. M. H.

Having defigned a Monumental Stone to be put up for HOLLAR, if this fmall Impreffion meets with a fuitable Encouragement; a Friend of mine fent the following Lines, though the Plate underneath was already engrav'd :

The Works of Nature and of Men,
By thee preferv'd, take Life again ;
And ev'n thy PRAGUE ferenely fhines,
Secure from Ravage in thy Lines.
In juft Return this Marble Frame
Would add fome Ages to thy Name :
Too frail, alas ! 'tis forc'd to own,
Thy SHADOWS will out-laft the STONE.

W. B.

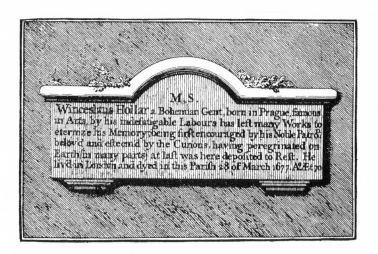

CONTENTS

LIST OF PLATES

All are from original etchings by Hollar, except those otherwise described.
Numbers of reference are to the catalogue in this volume, and to Parthey.

xi

WENCESLAUS HOLLAR

HOLLAR'S LIFE

WENCESLAUS[1] HOLLAR was born in Prague on the 13th July, 1607, *i. e.* just within a year after the birth of Rembrandt. He was the son of a lawyer in an official position, who is said to have suffered for his adherence to Frederick V, King of Bohemia, the unfortunate son-in-law of James I. So at least relates Aubrey,[2] who speaks from personal acquaintance with the etcher. But the elder Hollar appears to have remained in Prague until his death in 1630, and Wenceslaus did not leave his native city until 1627,[3] so that his own artistic inclination was more probably the reason for his departure than his father's political ruin after the Battle of Prague in 1619.

Aubrey also relates that Hollar told him how "when he was a school-boy he took a delight in drawing of maps," and he described the "draughts he kept" as "pretty." So the future etcher of

[1] This is the form generally used by Hollar when he signed in full; *Wenzel* is the German, *Václav* the Bohemian form. The most recent book on Hollar, partly based on research in England, L. J. Živný, *Václav Hollar, Nové příspévky k jeho životopisu* (New Contributions to his Life), Prague, 1911, I have been unable to consult through ignorance of the language.

[2] See p. 26, *The Chief Authorities consulted.*

[3] This and several details of his life are authenticated by the account probably supplied by the artist for the engraved inscription beneath his etching of himself after Meyssens (P. 1419), reproduced in my frontispiece.

The inscription reads: WENCESLAUS HOLLAR. *Gentilhomme ne a Prage l'an 1607. a esté de nature fort inclin pr l'art de meniature principalement pour esclaircir, mais beaucoup retardé par son pere, l'an 1627, il est party de Prage aijant demeure en divers lieux en Allemaigne, il ç est addonne pour peu de temps a esclaircir et aplicquer l'eau forte, estant party de Coloigne avec le Comte d'Arondel vers Vienne et dillée par Prage vers l'Angleterre, ou aijant esté serviteur domesticque du Duc de Jorck, il s'est retire de la a cause de la guerre a Anvers ou il reside encores.*

Ie. Meyssens pinxit et excudit.

B

topography was in the making at school, in spite of discouragement from his father, who intended him for the law.

A few of his etchings are dated in 1625 and 1626, several being copies of Dürer. They were thus done before he left Prague, and have the appearance of being the work of an amateur who had not yet received regular artistic training. Hollar's first regular instruction in the art of etching is said to have been under Matthäus Merian the elder, in Frankfort, for about two years from 1627, and he afterwards worked for a few years in Strassburg and Cologne.[1] One of the most attractive results of his residence in the former city is the small set of the *Seasons with Strassburg Views* (P. 622–625).

Vertue says that he had "difficulty enough to subsist" at Cologne, but his opportunity came with the advent of the Earl of Arundel. The famous collector was on an embassy to Ferdinand II in Vienna (which lasted from April till December 1636), and probably first became acquainted with Hollar's work when passing Cologne on his way out. He was sufficiently attracted to attach Hollar to his suite, the series of twenty-four small views published by Hollar in 1635, with the title *Amoenissimae aliquot Locorum Effigies*, being just the sort of work which may have inspired the Earl with the idea of engaging such an illustrator to commemorate his travels.

One of Hollar's small German views, that of Würzburg (P. 735) is definitely signed as done on the embassy: *W. Hollar delineavit A° 1636 in Legatione Arundeliana ad Imperatorem.*

William Crowne published in 1637 *A True Relation of all the Remarkable Places . . . observed in the Travels of the . . . Earle of Arundel . . . Ambassadour Extraordinary to . . . Ferdinando the Second . . .* 1636, and Nagler states that the book was illus-

---

[1] Vertue also refers to a journey to Antwerp at this period, without mentioning Strassburg. Perhaps he has confused the two. Inscriptions on his etchings (*i. e.* P. 751–755) show that he made drawings in Strassburg in 1629 and 1630. In his etchings he often uses drawings done many years earlier, giving the dates of each in several cases. *E. g.* the large *View of Prague*, etched at Antwerp in 1649 (P. 880), was based on a drawing done in 1636 when in the suite of the Earl of Arundel.

trated by Hollar. But none of the several copies of the book in the British Museum and at Windsor contains any plates, so that if the Earl had projected this illustration it does not seem to have been carried into execution. There is no reference to Wenceslaus Hollar in Crowne's text.

By the end of December 1636 Arundel reached home again, and in 1637 Hollar etched his first plates in England, *e.g.* the *View of Greenwich* (No. 203, Plates XXVIII and XXIX). Possibly the studio shown on the E. of the courtyard of Arundel House in the etching No. 83 (see Plate XLIX) may be the actual place where he worked. For the next few years he was busy etching plates after drawings and other works of art in the Earl's collection, and a considerable number of his London views also date before the Civil War.

With constant work for his patron as well as the printsellers, these early years in England must have been the time of Hollar's greatest success. Two of the most interesting books he helped to illustrate at this period were Puget de la Serre's *Histoire de l'Entrée de la Reyne Mère du Roy très Chrestien dans les . . . Pays Bas*, and his *Histoire de l'Entrée de la Reyne Mère . . . dans la Grande-Bretaigne*, both published in London in 1639. But it is curious that Hollar only seems to have done the allegorical and portrait plates for the introductory part of these volumes, and not the topographical and historical scenes for which his art was so fitted.[1]

Soon after his arrival Aubrey tells us that Hollar married "at Arundel House my ladies wayting woman, Mrs. Tracy, by whom he had a daughter, that was one of the greatest beauties I have seen ; his son by her dyed in the plague, an ingeniose youth ; drew delicately." Beyond that notice nothing is known of the son and his work. He may have assisted his father, as his mother is also reported to have done. At least Nagler refers to Hollar's wife helping the artist, *e.g.* in his series of *Muffs*.

[1] Compare p. 11.

About 1639 he was appointed a teacher of drawing in the Royal Household, probably to both the young Princes.[1] His view of *Richmond*, etched in 1638 (No. 109, Plate LVIII), shows the Prince of Wales with courtiers in the foreground (the barge from which they have disembarked bears his Feathers), so that Hollar was probably already known at Court in 1638.

Unhappily for Hollar the Earl of Arundel left England with other Royalist refugees in 1642, and it was about this time, no doubt, that Hollar was attached to the service of the Duke of York. In spite of the Civil Wars Hollar kept busily at work, doing as many as sixty-seven plates in 1643, and forty in 1644. In the latter year he and several other artists, among whom were Inigo Jones and William Faithorne, took up arms, and served under the Marquis of Winchester at Basing House. Robert Peake, the print-seller, who was actually second in command at Basing House, may have induced the engravers in his employ to join him. Hollar was taken prisoner in 1644 before the fall of Basing House, but managed to make his escape to Antwerp, where he joined his patron. In 1644 plates are dated both in London, and at Antwerp, and in the next year Hollar's name is found among the members of the Guild of St. Luke. Misfortune again met him, in the death of the Earl of Arundel, who had been ordered south for his health, and died at Padua in 1646. Thrown entirely on his own resources Hollar produced an enormous amount of work during the next six years at Antwerp, some 350 plates being dated between 1645 and 1651.

In 1652 Hollar returned to England,[2] and was soon busily

---

[1] Vertue thinks it was the Prince of Wales to whom he taught drawing, " having seen a small Portrait-Book with silver clasps mounting the Arms or Badge of the Prince of Wales, the Crown and Feathers : within this Book are several drawings, parts of the face and heads to begin to learn from, with Hollar's own hand-writing ; which book was in the possession of the Rt. Hon. the Earl of Oxford." I cannot find where this book is now. The *Dictionary of National Biography* is in error in inferring that it is among the Harleian MSS. in the British Museum.

[2] Aubrey adds a curious little personal reminiscence showing the foreign artist's

employed for the booksellers, etching numerous plates for the publications of Ogilby, Dugdale, Ashmole, and others. Two of his plates for Ogilby's *Virgil* (1654) are dated as etched in London in 1652. He was living in 1654 in the house of William Faithorne near Temple Bar, who was an active printseller as well as the most famous English line-engraver of the time. Hollar also appears to have lodged with other printsellers such as Peter Stent, and John Overton, working by the hour at small pay. According to his friend the amateur and etcher Francis Place,[1] " he had a method of working not common. He did all by the hour, in which he was very exact, for if anybody came in, and kept him from his business, he always laid the hourglass on one side, till they were gone. He always received 12^d an hour." And Peter Stent told Place that he only gave 30s. for the *View of Greenwich* (see No. 20), " which two plates," according to Vertue, " might fairly be worth five times as much."

Hollar celebrated the Restoration by one of his finest etchings, the *Coronation of Charles II in Westminster Abbey* (see No. 101, and Plate LVI). He again obtained some appointment at Court, that of the King's " Scenographer, or designer of prospects,"[2] but it did not greatly improve his fortunes. Charles at least helped

---

view of the sour English faces of the Commonwealth: "I remember he told me that when he first came into England (which was a serene time of peace) that the people, both poor and rich, did looke cheerfully, but at his returne, he found the countenances of the people all changed, melancholy, spightfull, as if bewitched."

[1] See letter, dated 1716, transcribed in Vertue MSS., Add. 21111, fol. 15.

[2] " Scenographer, or designer of prospects " is given in the " List of His Majesties Servants in Ordinary above Stairs " in E. Chamberlayne, *Present State of England*, 2nd ed. 1669, p. 267. I do not find *Scenographus Regis* added to Hollar's signature except in plates dated from 1672 (*e. g.* P. 993 and 995). He calls himself His Majesties Designer on the title to the *Views of Tangiers*, published 1673 (P. 1187). The *Interior of St. George's Chapel* (my No. 125) etched in 1663, is signed in the first state *W. Hollar delin: et sculp. 1663*. The addition *Scenographus Regis* was only made in the second state as used in Ashmole's *Garter*, 1672. The *Dictionary of National Biography* probably has authority in stating that he was sworn King's " Scenographer " on the 21st November, 1666.

him indirectly by writing to the Lord Mayor in 1660, requesting the aldermen and well-disposed citizens to contribute towards the expenses of a large map of London, then incomplete through lack of funds.[1]   The Corporation assisted Hollar on this and several other occasions.

Hollar married again in 1665, and had several children by his second wife.[2]   But his material fortune must have greatly suffered during the time of the Plague and the Fire, when there was little money to spare for the artist.   At this time according to Vertue, he was living in Bloomsbury.   He appealed to the King for pecuniary aid in 1667, but no definite work seems to have been given him until 1668–1669, when he was sent by the Government with Lord Henry Howard to Tangiers, to make sketches of the town and its fortifications,[3] a work of more than a year, for which he only received £100.   On the return voyage their ship only narrowly escaped capture by Algerine pirates, an action of which Hollar etched a plate for Ogilby's *Africa*, 1670 (*Captain Kempthorn's Engagement in the Mary Rose with seven Algerine Men-of-war*, see Plate III).   Hollar produced a fair number of plates for the booksellers during the last six years of his life (*e. g.* for Ashmole's *Institution of the Order of the Garter*, 1672, the third volume of Dugdale's *Monasticon*, 1673, Thoroton's *Nottinghamshire*, and Sandford's *Genealogical History*, 1677), but his diligence apparently failed to keep him from distress.

Vertue ends his biography with these words: " Hollar thus having led a painful and laborious life, always attended with

[1] Either the large map of Ogilby and Morgan (published 1677), my No. 14, or even more probably the map of which the piece covering the West Central District alone was completed (No. 6).

[2] Honora Hollar, as she signs herself in a deed of 25th May, 1677, relating to the residue of Hollar's estate (No. 68 in Mr. P. M. Barnard's Catalogue 41 of 1911, and now in the possession of Mr. Charles Whibley).

[3] Resulting in fifteen plates (P. 1187–1201).   The original drawings are now in the British Museum.   See E. M. G. Routh, *Tangier, England's lost Atlantic Outpost 1661–1684.   Engravings and Drawings after W. Hollar, etc.* London, 1912.   8°.

difficulties, reach'd to the age of seventy years, at which time he liv'd in Gardiner's Lane in Westminster, where he dy'd, but so indigent, that there was an execution in his House; of which, when he was dying, he was sensible enough to desire only to die in his bed, and not to be remov'd till he was buried, which was to the New Chapel Church-yard, Westminster, where he was interr'd."

The burial registers of St. Margaret's, Westminster, give the entry on the 28th March, 1677, ✠ *Wenceslaws Hollar* ✠ (with *the famous* added in a smaller hand immediately below),[1] so that Aubrey, who further states that he was buried in St. Margaret's churchyard near the north-west corner of the tower, is probably correct in giving Lady-day, the 25th March, as the date of his death.

His industry and conscientious methods of work of themselves bear witness to one side of Hollar's personality, and pleasant touches are added by Aubrey's description of him as "a friendly good-natured man as could be, but shiftlesse as to the world," and by the "very honest, simple, well-meaning man" of John Evelyn. They are enough to explain Hollar's distresses even when he had no apparent lack of commissions.

---

[1] I am told that the cross against the name implies that the burial service was performed by a bishop, so that with all his poverty Hollar was thought much of. It is the rarest thing for any personal note to follow the names in the registers, so the clerk's addition of *the famous* means a great deal. I have verified the above entry, but cannot find any reference to his burial as being in the *New Chappel burying ground* (whatever that was) as given by Vertue on fol. 28 of his MS. notes, British Museum, Add. 23070.

HOLLAR'S WORK

"IF anyone want truth without pretention let him go to Hollar. If he want perfection of 'biting' and the precise degree of gradation required, let him also go to Hollar. If he want to live in the time illustrated, let him again go to Hollar. . . . People sometimes say to me, 'What is it you see in Hollar?' and I always answer, 'Not quite, but nearly everything.' The 'Shells' are a marvel of colour, and of handling; and the 'Nave of St. George's Chapel,' as to *gradations* and *finesse*, the most wonderful piece of 'biting' known to me . . . the simple probity of the man fascinates me. . . ." These words of Sir Francis Seymour Haden[1] carry great weight as of one who was at once a most excellent etcher and the most critical of connoisseurs. Haden's own style possessed a freedom and breadth entirely alien to Hollar's genius, and this very dissimilarity adds weight to the etcher's appreciation.

Hollar, with his wonderful command over his material, might very truly be called the etcher's etcher, and I can well believe that another completely dissimilar spirit, the great Rembrandt himself, admired his contemporary with the same warmth as Seymour Haden. No words of appreciation are extant, but Rembrandt's etching of the *Shell* seems to me to contain this appreciation materialised. There is no signature, date, or title

[1] *About Etching:* London (Fine Art Society), 1879. Etchers may be interested to refer to a detailed description of "Mr. Wenceslaus Hollar's ground for Etching in copper or brass; with his directions how to use it" in Vertue's Catalogue, 1759, p. 133. The reference to brass, which must have been frequently used by early engravers instead of copper, is interesting. A still earlier article on "how to make Mr. Hollar's ground" occurs in *The Excellency of the Pen and Pencil*, printed by Dorman Newman, London, 1688 (Book II. chap. i.).

on any of Hollar's shells (a series of thirty-eight plates), but we are probably right in assuming that they were done before 1650, the date of Rembrandt's etching. Vertue states that they were the last work done by Hollar from objects in the Earl of Arundel's collection. It is possible, on that account, that Hollar was unable to afford their publication after the Earl's death. In any case they are among the rarest of Hollar's works. None of Hollar's shells shows a background, and there is no aim at picturesqueness. In fact, they might have been intended for some conchological work, though they were never so used. If there are touches of the graver on these plates, they are of the fewest. Hollar always shows the most remarkable delicacy in his use of the etched line, but here he achieves in addition a brilliance which, in etching, is even more remarkable than delicacy of work (see Plate IV).

Rembrandt's *Shell* must, I think, have been inspired by the sight of Hollar's work. Only Rembrandt, while preserving a wonderfully faithful and detailed imitation, shows himself the painter in the background of dark shadow in which the shell is set.

No less remarkable than the shells for the virtuosity of their etching are the *Butterflies* (of which the majority were dated in 1646 and 1647), and *Muffs* (dated between 1642 and 1647), one of which is reproduced on Plate IV. In view of the minute perfection of Hollar's plates, it is strange to read that he practically only had the use of one eye. His friend, the amateur etcher Francis Place, in the letter from which we have already quoted,[1] wrote that "he had a defect in one of his eyes, which was the left, so that he always held his hand before it when he wrought; he never used spectacles . . ."

Hollar's work is both varied and extensive, more than 2700 plates being described in the standard catalogue of Parthey. It embraces landscape, topography, costume, portraits, scripture,

[1] See above, p. 5.

history, mythology, allegory, emblems, natural history, repro-
ductions of old paintings, drawings and goldsmith's work,
heraldry, and book illustrations of all kinds.

The Earl of Arundel was one of the earliest collectors to
conceive the idea of recording his collection by reproducing its
greatest treasures on copper, and the diversity of Hollar's work
of reproduction, of paintings, drawings, goldsmith's work and
what not, was partly the outcome of his work for his patron.
As an etcher of history and subjects with numerous figures, he
was always incisive and vivid in his drawing, without the
brilliant and piquant qualities of his French contemporary Jacques
Callot. But Hollar kept far more purely to the use of the etching
needle than Callot, who added emphasis and brilliance to his
etched lines by means of the graver.

A considerable number of Hollar's historical prints were done
early in his life, when little illustrations of the exciting events of
the Civil Wars were in great demand. Among the best are the
Trial and *Execution of Strafford* (Nos. 91 and 23, Plates LIII
and XXXI), but several of his smaller and less important plates
are peculiarly interesting. A series of these was used to illustrate
John Vicars *A Sight of the Transactions of these latter yeares
emblemized with engraven plats which men may read without
spectacles* [London, 1646], and the two later editions issued under
the title *True Information of the Beginning and Cause of all our
Troubles* [1648-1649].[1] How little Hollar, or rather his publisher,
cared for historical truth, as long as he gave an illustration which
would reasonably fit the event, is seen in the way in which the same
print is made to do service in the different editions for different
subjects.

Another set of small historical illustrations, the *Solemn League
and Covenant*, forms a small pamphlet with both text and illustrations in etching. The whole series of title and seven subjects
is etched on one copper plate, and the impressions were taken from

[1] See Nos. 24, 25, 31, 87, 93, 108, and Plate XXXIII.

the separate sections with the other parts blocked out.   If a single
impression had been taken and then cut into its sections, the
subjects would only have had margins on two sides at the most,
and margins would be essential as the subjects were probably
issued bound or stitched as a pamphlet (see No. 89 and Plate
LIII).   These early historical prints are etched for the most part in
a lighter and more open manner than his topographical prints or
figure subjects.   The difference of style is so distinct that one is
almost tempted to take a further step, and consider the possibility
of his having etched the unsigned topographical and historical
plates in the books of Puget de la Serre, 1639, to which we have
already referred.[1]   But there is a looseness of drawing about these
plates (of which the *Progress of Marie de Medicis along Cheapside*
is the most pertinent to our theme) which is so inferior to the
slightest of Hollar's accepted historical subjects, that we should
probably err in considering the attribution.

Among the most interesting of his historical prints are the
Sea-battles, e. g. the *Action of Prince Rupert against the Dutch,
on 9th and 10th August*, 1666 (P. 1246), and *Capt. Kempthorn's
Engagement in the Mary Rose with seven Algerine Men-of-war*
(see Plate III).   The latter has already been mentioned in the
section on Hollar's life, as the artist was himself in the *Mary Rose*
on his return voyage from Algiers when she was attacked by these
pirates.   Even more attractive than these purely marine subjects is
the *View of the Spanish, Dutch and English Fleets off Deal*, as they
were ranged before an engagement, 1640 (P. 548).   It is a long
subject on two plates, about the same shape and size as the *View
of Greenwich* (No. 1, Plates XXVIII and XXIX), and the coast-
line with its houses, fort and onlookers makes a delightful picture
with the picturesque background of the fleets and their forest of
masts drawn with no wasted detail, and in their delicately etched
line so perfectly attuned to their distance from the spectator.   Even
Callot's naval subjects, such as the *Siege of the Fort St. Martin*

---

[1] See above, p. 3.

de Ré, seem hard beside the sensitive touch and subtle atmosphere of a print like this.

Hollar was also a fairly prolific recorder of the history of his time in portrait. Occasionally he produced an original portrait, such as that of *William Dugdale* (see Plate V), which appeared as frontispiece to Dugdale's *Antiquities of Warwickshire* (1656) and *History of St. Paul's Cathedral* (1658), but most of Hollar's portrait work was reproductive. He was at his strongest in the *James II as Duke of York*, after Teniers (1651, see Plate VI), but many others could be cited which show real vigour combined with his unfailing delicacy of execution. The oval portrait of *Charles I*, after Van Dyck, which is also reproduced (catalogue, No. 92, Plate I), is not only one of the most excellent, but of particular interest to our subject because of the attractive background formed of Whitehall, Westminster, and the River. The *Inigo Jones* (Plate V) is another good example after Van Dyck, and raises some surprise at Vertue's statement that he was no favourite of Van Dyck, "because he could not so well enter into that master's true manner of drawing." Still one has to admit that Hollar was lacking in the virility of style that characterises Paul Pontius, Lucas Vorsterman, and several others of the best engravers of Van Dyck portraits.

Hollar certainly lacked something of the fire that goes to make the great engraver of portrait or life. His best work was in the faithful rendering of nature in her impersonal manifestations, whether in landscape, topography, costume, or in the still life, such as the shells and muffs to which allusion has already been made.

His etchings of costume are among the most exquisite of their kind. There is the set of twenty-seven plates including the etched title *Ornatus Muliebris Anglicanus or the Severall Habits of English Women, from the Nobilitie to the contry Women* . . . 1640, and the more extensive series of smaller plates issued first with the title *Theatrum Mulierum* 1643, and later as *Aula Veneris* . . .

1644. This second series, which in still later editions included a hundred plates illustrating English and Foreign costume, is certainly the most attractive of the two, and one of the title pages and three subjects are reproduced on Plate VII. The *English Noble-woman* (P. 1883) is after Van Dyck,[1] but most of these figures were drawn from the life as well as etched by Hollar.

The charming set of *Female heads in circles* (P. 1908–1944) is also more essentially a series of costume than of portrait studies, though they are attractive in the latter relation as well. As costume again one must regard the two sets of the *Seasons*, illustrated in female figures, full-length in one set (P. 606–609), and three-quarter length in the other (P. 610–613). The *Seasons* in full-length figures are extremely rare in fine impressions, and one of them, the *Winter* (P. 609, No. 30 in my catalogue), is of particular interest to my subject in giving a view of Cornhill and the old Exchange in the background (Plate VIII). The *Summer* (P. 607, No. 97 below) also shows a London view, St. James's Park with Whitehall and St. Paul's in the distance, but hardly one of equal interest to the *Winter*.[2]

Finally we come to Hollar's topography; by far the most important part of his work.

From the end of the fifteenth century, with the increasing interest shown in discovery and travel in general, there was a growing demand for printed maps and views. Excellently engraved maps had appeared in an edition of Ptolemy's Geography, printed by Arnold Buckinck at Rome in 1478. They are as finely and precisely engraved as any of the maps engraved a century later by

---

[1] Also signed as after Van Dyck is a second version of the *English noblewoman in winter attire* (P. 1884) in the British Museum, not described by Parthey.

[2] It has been suggested to me by Mr. Aleck Abrahams that the Elizabethan house in the background of the *Spring* (P. 606) is Parsloes, at Dagenham, near Barking, the ancient seat of the Fanshawes, but I can find no illustrative evidence. The ruins on the river bank in the background of the *Autumn* (P. 608) of the same series might also be on the Thames in the neighbourhood of London. I have not included either in my catalogue.

the great geographer Gerard Mercator, who was his own engraver, Frans Hogenberg, who worked for Ortelius,[1] or Jodocus Hondius, chiefly interesting to English students for his splendid series of engraved county maps in John Speed's *Theatre of the Empire of Great Britain*, 1611. Characteristic of all these earlier map engravers is the attempt to add some pictorial elements to the chart: faces for the winds, ships at sea, nymphs for the rivers, a great variety of allegorical figures, and constant attempts to represent the appearance of towns rather than keep to the abstract conventions which satisfy the more scientific modern geographer. In his maps of countries and counties Hollar was already on the modern side. There are no longer the river-nymphs and spirits of the hills that appear in William Hole's maps to Michael Drayton's *Polyolbion*, 1613, though that is less typical of the saner cartography of the period, than an extreme example of the fantastic treatment of a poet dabbling in topography. But Hollar's touch, his method of indicating hills, and his very manner of writing with the needle have a distinction quite apart from his contemporary map-engravers of the middle and later seventeenth century in England. It is enough to compare his county maps in *Speed's Maps Epitomiz'd*, 1681,[2] with those engraved by R. Palmer for the same series, to see the difference between the true artist and the craftsman clearly showing in work that might be regarded as quite outside the realm of the painter-etcher.

In plans of towns Hollar kept for the most part closer to the old conventional lines than in his country and county maps. Here again the tradition was pictorial, as opposed to the modern abstract convention. The plan was practically always a bird's-eye view. In the case of small plans covering large towns, Hollar probably cared little more than his predecessors for faithful adherence to the

---

[1] F. Hogenberg was also responsible for the engraving of many of the attractive views (chiefly bird's-eye) in Georg Braun's famous publication, *Civitates Orbis Terrarum* (Cologne, about 1572–1618).

[2] See p. 30 and Nos. 1, 2, 3 and 111 of our catalogue.

detail of architecture—it would, in fact, be practically impossible to reproduce the buildings of a town on so minute a scale (*e. g.* the *Map of London before the Fire*, reproduced in Plate XI). He no doubt only aimed at clothing the skeleton of streets in an architectural dress that would give the general characteristics of the place in question, and satisfy at once the lover of the old traditions of plan-making and his own pictorial instinct.

On the other hand, in his larger bird's-eye plans, such as that of the *West Central District of London* (No. 6 below, and Plate XIV), Hollar certainly aimed at giving the semblance of an exact rendering of all the buildings in the district, though it is doubtful whether any but the most important houses were really drawn with accuracy. This particular plan, only known in the British Museum impression, is a real masterpiece in its combination of the practical aims of a map and the most attractive delineation conceivable of the houses and gardens of the city. It is full of atmosphere and charm as a picture of Gothic London, and etched in Hollar's most exquisite style.

The most striking predecessor of Hollar's bird's-eye plan is the large plan of Bruges, etched on ten plates by Marcus Gheraerts the elder, in 1562. This Marcus Gheraerts was the father of the famous portrait painter of the late Elizabethan and early Jacobean period, who is more generally known in the anglicised form of his name, Mark Garrard. Gheraerts the elder, who settled as a refugee in England at the time of the Alvan persecutions in 1568, is also the author of a series of etchings representing a *Procession of the Knights of the Order of the Garter* in 1576, which is only known in two impressions, one at the British Museum, and another, a mutilated set, in the Heralds' College. The plates are unsigned, and their authorship is only established by the reduced copy done by Hollar as an illustration to Elias Ashmole's *Order of the Garter* (1672), a copy which is referred to in my catalogue (No. 117), as it contains a view of *Windsor Castle*. But these plates, though extremely interesting as an illustration of English costume, would hardly prepare one for the real beauty of the plan of Bruges, which is almost the only sixteenth-century bird's-eye plan which I would place on a level with Hollar's.

The one important example in which Hollar discarded the bird's-eye convention in his plans of towns is his *Large Map of London*, based on Ogilby and Morgan's survey, 1677 (No. 14 in my list). Immediately after the Fire John Ogilby and William Morgan were appointed by the Corporation to map out disputed properties, and they subsequently undertook a more complete survey, showing both streets and houses, of the whole city. This was the survey etched at least in part by Hollar,[1] and published by William Morgan after Ogilby's death. Even here, with all the accuracy and the conventions of the modern map, Hollar did not fail to add charming pieces of illustration in details of the river banks and its shipping.

A very large number of Hollar's most attractive views of towns were etched as borders to his plans, in compartments along the top, or at the sides. But his avowedly practical purpose seldom rendered either picture or plan pedestrian in character. On a much larger and more imposing scale Piranesi started out to illustrate his archeological and architectural theories, never hesitating to annotate his plates with letter and number of reference to his text. He, too, never fails to render one forgetful of his antiquarian purpose, under the sway of his magnificent and inspiring design. Thus we have one of the most picturesque of Hollar's views of London on the same plate as his *Map of London* of 1675 (see No. 13 below), and splendid views of *London on Fire* both on the *Map of Great Britain and Ireland* (P. 648, see No. 7 (*b*) below), and on the *Exact Surveigh of the streets contained within the ruins of the city of London*, of 1669 (see No. 12, and Plates XII and XIII). This *Exact Surveigh*, one of three prints by Hollar showing the extent of the devastation caused by the Great Fire, is stated in its inscription to have been reduced from a larger map by John Leake on six

[1] See more detailed notes in catalogue, No. 14.

plates published in December 1666. Further reference is given to this matter in the catalogue, but it is strange that all traces of this larger survey, if it was ever actually engraved, have disappeared.

Hollar's artistic pedigree in landscape and architectural etching is by no means difficult to trace. Matthäus Merian the elder, under whom he studied in Frankfort, was his immediate inspirer in a style that went back to the Italianised Flemish School of landscape etching, of which the Brueghels, and Paul Bril, were the chief representatives. Their precision and charm of line descended to Hollar unalloyed, but shorn of most of the quaint affectations that characterised their work. Hollar still kept in view the decorative, as opposed to the merely natural treatment of landscape, but in general he was infinitely more simple and direct in his translation of nature. The very best of Merian's work is bald and dry in comparison with Hollar's developed style. It is completely without Hollar's magical touch, and his sense of atmosphere and aerial perspective. Some of Hollar's charm of manner may lie with what might be called his roundness of style : an affection like Dürer's and Rowlandson's for the round curving lines, which are so comfortable an element in the work of both of these masters. Hollar is nearest to Merian in some of his foreign views, probably the earlier of these plates, *e. g.* the *View and Plan of Rostock* (P. 885). Another plate left by Parthey under Hollar's name, the *View and Plan of Ratisbon* (P. 881) must, I think, be etched entirely by Merian, the drawing of the view alone, as the signature indicates, being by Hollar.

In Hollar's smaller landscapes one still feels a close relation to such plates of Merian's as the *Novae regionum aliquot amœnissimarum delineationes* (1624). But Hollar developed to a much more remarkable extent the most delicate gradations in the strength of line to express wonderful effects of distance in plates of the smallest compass. Some of the most exquisite of these small plates are in the series published at Cologne in 1635, with the title *Amoenissimae aliquot Locorum Effigies*, and even more astonishing

c

is the little view of *Unter-Assaw* (P. 896), but there are equally beautiful examples among his small English views, particularly those of Surrey and Sussex. In Surrey he did a charming series of six plates *by Albury* where his patron, the Earl of Arundel, had a country house. One of the set is dated at Antwerp, 1645, but he must have based his etching on earlier drawings. Several of the smaller London views show an equal quality in the wonderfully delicate line, notably three of the six *Islington views* with the city in the distance (Nos. 73, 75 and 77, and Plates XLV and XLIV), and the delightful view of *London from the top of Arundel House* (No. 81, Plate XLVIII). But more masterly and magical still is the long view of *Greenwich* on two plates (No. 20, Plates XXVIII and XXIX) with the winding river and its shipping, the distant towers of London, and the low line of hills beyond. This plate, etched in 1637, is interesting for the change of lettering, which seems an indication of the temper of the time. The first state shows a long dedication to Queen Henrietta Maria, which was erased to make place for some non-committal verses in praise of the scene by Henry Peacham. So very few impressions of the first state are known, that one concludes Hollar or his publisher feared that the unpopularity of the Court at this date would militate against the sale of a print with the Royal dedication.

The majority of Hollar's etchings of topography are original, but there is still a very considerable number based on drawings by others. For example, nearly all the views done for Thoroton's *Antiquities of Nottinghamshire* (1677) were after drawings by a Richard Hall. Then one of the views of *Windsor Castle* (see No. 116 below, and Plate LVIII) was etched after a drawing by Sir Christopher Wren—one wonders where such drawings by Wren are, and whether, if in existence, they would be attributed to him. And Van Dyck's, moreover, is the drawing of the little *View of Rye* on the *Map of Kent* (P. 665), etched by Hollar, and prefixed to Thomas Philipott's *Villane Kantianum* (1659). It reminds one of the intensely beautiful landscape sketches in pen and ink, water-colour, and body-colour, which so few people think of in connexion with Van Dyck.

Two of Hollar's little London views, those of the Court-yard of Arundel House, are signed as based on the drawings of Adam Alexius Bierling. Practically nothing is known of this Adam Bierling beyond his name on Hollar's etchings—on several of the others dating between 1646 and 1650, he appears as the publisher or printer (*A. A. Bierling excudit*). Two of them bear a dedication from Bierling (one dated at Antwerp, 1646), so that he was probably Hollar's employer, and not merely Hollar's printer. In fact, Hollar probably never really became an etcher who could command his market: he seems always to have worked as the drudge of publishers and printers. Only on one of his many prints (the *Charles II* after Van Dyck, P. 1442; see No. 95 below, and Plate II) is his name predicated with *excudit* (*i. e.* printed or published) in addition to *fecit* (etched). Hollar probably had no drawings of Arundel House of his own in Antwerp, and Bierling was, no doubt, freer at this period to visit England.

Even Hollar's greatest London plate, the *Long Bird's-eye View of London from Bankside* (No. 16, Plates XV–XX) was etched away from the spot during his residence at Antwerp in 1647. No doubt Hollar possessed many drawings of the subject, or of parts of the subject, done before he left England a few years before, but it is also quite possible that in developing the view on his plate he may have had recourse in detail to drawings by others, perhaps even by Bierling, though in this case it was not Bierling, but the better-known Cornelis Danckers, who published the plate. In the general arrangement of the whole view he may also have depended on Visscher's famous print of 1616. There are many discrepancies in details of architecture between Visscher's and Hollar's views, far more than can be excused by the interval that elapsed between the two publications. In general I should be inclined to accept Hollar's as the truer to detail. He had, of course, had more opportunity of original sketching in London. Apart from this view signed *C. J.*

Visscher delineavit, which must, I think, denote a drawing taken on the spot, there is no indication that the Amsterdam publisher and etcher Claesz Jansz Visscher did other work in London.[1]

But even granting so much, Hollar was probably not so far in advance of his times as to be greatly troubled about accuracy of detail. I can imagine that picturesqueness of presentation was always his prior aim. For a general idea of what London looked like at this period there could be no securer guide than Hollar. Apart from his diligent sketching from nature, and his study of the city's architecture, every plate that he did is redolent of the atmosphere of his adopted city. It cannot be said that Hollar invariably succeeded in giving the local colour of the countries he portrayed, but where he failed it was always owing to lack of firsthand knowledge. One does not expect his drawings of the East to contain the Oriental flavour. It is perhaps more surprising to note how little Italian are his Italian views. His Italian towns, none of which he had seen, are hopelessly hybrid reflections of Northern and Southern architecture. But these failures serve to throw into relief the perfection of his views in Germany, the Netherlands, and England.

Many of his original drawings are preserved. Most of them are in pen and ink, and in style like his etchings in their delicacy and precision. The more finished are generally brushed with light and transparent washes of water-colour ; for example, the view of *Whitehall from the Thames* (L. B. 10), and the *Tower of London* (L. B. 9), in the British Museum (see Plate IX).[2] Another Museum drawing reproduced, the *View*

---

[1] Visscher's view in its earliest state (British Museum, King's Library) is dated on letterpress at the foot *Amstelodami ex Officina Judoci Hondii . . . Anno 1616*. This still leaves the question of engraver unsolved, as Jodocus Hondius is generally supposed to have died in 1612, so that it may be one of the engravers who succeeded to his workshop (Justus or Hendrik Hondius?). On the other hand Visscher may have been the etcher as well as draughtsman. For a long account of this view, see T. F. Ordish, *London Topographical Record* (London Topographical Society), VI. (1909), p. 39.

[2] For description of these and other drawings by Hollar in the British Museum, see

of the Thames at Westminster seen from the Quay at Lambeth House (L. B. 11, Plate IX), is one of his most excellent drawings in pen and ink. There are traces of pencil or black chalk beneath the ink lines, showing his method of starting his sketch. Occasionally he used silver point, as in a little *View of Hampton Court with a Design for a Sun-dial* (L. B. 8), also in the Museum. The British Museum possesses altogether nearly fifty drawings by Hollar, including the series done at Tangiers in 1668–1669. Other drawings in the British Museum touching our subject are the little sketch of *Richmond Palace* (L. B. 12), probably a study for the etching (No. 109), and a large drawing in pen and ink and water-colour, on vellum, of the *Quadrangle in Windsor Castle* (L. B. 30). The latter, like the Tangiers series, is almost too large to suit Hollar's style, and lacks the subtlety, both in line and wash, that gives his drawings their delicate flavour. One of the drawings, lettered *bey Gravesand in England* (L. B. 13), is signed *W H* (in mongram) 1623. If the signature and date are genuine, and they are not beyond question, Hollar must have made a visit to England long before what is generally regarded as his first arrival in 1636–1637. In any case, the drawing has all the marks of an early work in its somewhat uncertain and tentative touch.

Another very beautiful drawing of London, *Westminster Abbey and part of Westminster from the River*, was in the collection of Mr. J. P. Heseltine,[1] but I cannot refer to its present locality. It is in pen and ink washed with water-colour, in the same manner as the drawings of the Tower and Whitehall in the British Museum.

In the Royal Library at Windsor Castle there are two drawings of interest to our subject, a charming little sketch

---

Laurence Binyon, *Catalogue of Drawings by British Artists and Artists of Foreign Origin working in England*, Vol. II. 1900.

[1] Reproduced as No. 24, in *Original Drawings, chiefly of the German school in the collection of J. P. H.* Privately printed: London, 1912.

in pen and ink and water-colour of *Richmond*,[1] and a *View of the Thames looking towards the North Bank, with the Savoy, Somerset House, and Old St. Paul's in the distance*,[2] executed in pencil and pen and ink.

A more numerous series of Hollar's drawings is in the Pepys Library, Magdalene College, Cambridge. They are pasted in the first volume of the *Collection of Prints and Drawings relating to London*, brought together by Samuel Pepys, and arranged in large folio volumes in 1700.[3] There are ten[4] drawings certainly by Hollar, and three more which might be his work, though by no means up to his usual standard. They are all in pen and ink, for the most part slight sketches, and none in the more finished style with water-colour wash. The most interesting is a study for the etching of *London by Milford Staires* (Pepys, I. p. 240, *b*), which is reproduced on Plate X (see also remarks in the catalogue below, No. 80). Another of the slighter sketches, that of the *Savoy Palace* (Pepys, I. p. 237, *d*), seems to have formed the basis of the etching, No. 84. A third, a *View of the Banqueting Hall, Whitehall, and Holbein's Gate* (Pepys, I. p. 98) (which was engraved and published in 1809 by William Herbert and Robt. Wilkinson[5]) is very similar in its point of view to a rare etching of Israel Silvestre.[6] Besides these, the most attractive are two views of *Westminster Abbey* (Pepys, I. pp. 187, *a*, and 188, *a*), one of the West Front with a coach in the foreground being particularly

[1] An entirely different subject from the etching of *Richmond* (No. 109), *q. v.*

[2] See note under etching of the *West Central District* (No. 6).

[3] See W. R. Lethaby, "Pepys London Collection," *London Topographical Record* (London Topographical Society), Vol. II. (1903), p. 66.

[4] Eleven, including the drawing of *St. Pancras Church* (Pepys, I. p. 119), described as by Hollar in Pepys's index. I add this here as I failed to note it in looking through the volume, and so can offer no opinion.

[5] Published later in *Londina Illustrata* (R. Wilkinson), 1819, I., pl. 87. Reproduced in the *London Topographical Record* (London Topographical Society), VI. (1909), p. 35.

[6] An engraved copy of the Silvestre plate was published by W. Herbert, 1808, and later in *Londina Illustrata* (R. Wilkinson), 1819, I., pl. 86.

delightful (Plate X), and a small sketch of *London viewed from Southwark*, dated 1638 (Pepys, I. p. 31).

For the rest there are four slight sketches of different houses, (*a*) *Suffolk House*, (*b*) *York House*, (*c*) *Durham House, Salisbury House, Worcester House*, (*f*) *Somerset House*, the letters referring to the place in Pepys, I. p. 237, in which they occur with the drawing and etching of the *Savoy* already mentioned. The three doubtful drawings, not specified as by Hollar in Pepys's index, which might be by some weaker contemporary, are two of *Hampton Court*, from the river and land sides (Pepys, I. p. 209, *a* and *b*), and a small sketch of *Lambeth House* (Pepys, I. p. 224, *b*).

Two of the greatest collections of Hollar's etchings are happily in England, the Royal Collection in Windsor Castle and that of the British Museum being almost equally representative and rich in fine impressions. Vertue states in his *Description of the Works of Hollar* (1759, p. 150) that Hollar's widow survived him, and several years afterwards sold a large book of his works to Sir Hans Sloane, Bart. This, then, we may take to have formed the basis of the superb National Collection of Hollar's work.

A considerable number of Hollar's plates were printed in large numbers by various publishers[1] long after the master's death, so

[1] Hollar's chief contemporary publishers, whose names often appear on his prints, were Peter Stent (about 1643–1667 ; at the sign of the Crown, later of the White Horse, in Gilt Spur Street, without Newgate), and his successor John Overton (about 1667–1703, at the same address). So that prints bearing Stent or John Overton's address are often good early impressions (*e.g.* No. 19 below ; and No. 20, still good in state IV. with Stent's address). John Overton was succeeded by Henry Overton, who published a catalogue in partnership with John Hoole in 1734, and Henry Overton's name alone occurs on Hollar as late as 1742 (the set of *Sea-storms*, P. 1273–1276). Some of Overton's stock apparently passed into the hands of Robert Sayer, of 53 Fleet Street (who issued a catalogue in 1766 and was still publishing in 1787), and later to his successors Laurie and Whittle (see Nos. 19 and 20), who sold their stock of Hollar (146 numbers, to judge from a title page quoted by Parthey) in one folio volume at a guinea, as well as the separate prints at various prices from sixpence to four shillings (see Laurie and Whittle's catalogue 1795). R. H. Laurie issued a catalogue from the same address in Fleet Street in 1824. There are also some valueless Hollar impressions, generally on thin white paper, in " A Collection of Two Hundred Original Etchings "

that there is an enormous variety in the quality of different impressions. Amateurs must beware of judging his work from these later prints, and should always search for the early impressions. At present even the rarest of Hollar's prints in their finest states practically never fetch more than £20, and the smaller and commoner examples a few pounds at the most, so that the ordinary collector will find no insuperable difficulties in getting together a really attractive selection of his works at comparatively little expense.

Hollar had a good many followers, several amateurs like Francis Place and Daniel King among them, but few who did him much honour except perhaps Richard Gaywood. Gaywood was best in his portraits, but in any ambitious subject, such as the *Progress of Charles II to Parliament* (1661), he was thoroughly stiff in his figures and entirely without his master's charm of manner.

One of Hollar's worthiest successors in the etching of topography in England was Jan Kip, who did the plates for Strype's 1720 edition of Stow's *Survey of London*, and many bird's-eye views of the Royal Palaces and miscellaneous country houses for the *Britannia Illustrata* (or *Le Noveau Théatre de la Grande Bretagne*), published in various editions between 1707 and 1724. He followed Hollar's manner of etching and succeeded in retaining something of its true flavour. It is only necessary to compare the much harder line-engravings by Sutton Nicholls for the 1756 edition of Stow's *Survey*, to appreciate the peculiar attractiveness of the two earlier etchers. But Kip never possessed the subtlety in execution or the pictorial sense of Hollar. In this respect Hollar's tradition was continued with truer spirit by the Dutch historical etcher,

---

by Rembrandt and others, issued by various publishers between 1816 and 1826. A "Collection of forty-nine plates, engraved by Hollar, for Dugdale's *Monasticon* and *History of St. Paul's Cathedral*. Republished 1815, folio," is cited by Lowndes (*Bibliographer's Manual of English Literature*). They were probably taken from the original plates, which may be still in the possession of the Dugdale family.

Romeyn de Hooghe (1645–1708).[1] Kip's largest view, *A Prospect of the City of London, Westminster, and St. James's Park*, not only serves to show his deficiencies in comparison with Hollar, but offers a most instructive picture of the gulf that divides his London of the early years of the eighteenth century from the Gothic town of Hollar's etchings before the Great Fire.

[1] And not unworthily in some of the best bird's-eye views (bearing the address of F. de Wit, Amsterdam) in Pieter van der Aa's monumental work, *La Galérie Agréable du Monde* (Leyden, about 1730).

THE CHIEF AUTHORITIES CONSULTED

AUBREY, John. "Brief Lives," chiefly of contemporaries, set down by John Aubrey, between the years 1669 and 1696. Edited from the author's MSS. by Andrew Clark. 2 vols. Oxford. 1898. The most authoritative edition of Aubrey's "Lives."

For Life of Hollar, see Vol. I. p. 407, and also another reference on p. 301.

VERTUE, George. MSS. preserved in the British Museum. The chief material is in Add. 23082, fol. 48, etc., and Egerton 2384, the latter giving the "Life" in a more finished form. See also Add. 21111, fol. 15, for copy of a letter by Francis Place about Hollar (dated May 20, 1716); Add. 23075, fol. 80, etc., for a short biography; Add. 23085, fol. 40, for notes on his journey with the Earl of Arundel, and Add. 23070, fol. 28, for transcript from Registers of St. Margaret's, Westminster. Vertue published his material in the following editions:—

VERTUE, George. A Description of the Works of the Ingenious Delineator and Engraver Wenceslaus Hollar disposed into Classes of Different Sorts with some account of his Life. London, 1745. 4°.

Second Edition, with additions, 1759. The entries are numbered in the second edition (but not in the first), so that the references in our catalogue are to this edition.

CATALOGUE OF THE COLLECTION OF JOHN BARNARD. Sale, 16 April, 1798, and following days. London, 1798. Contains 325 lots by Hollar.

CATALOGUE OF A CAPITAL COLLECTION OF PRINTS, THE WORK OF THAT IN-COMPARABLE ARTIST, WENCESLAUS HOLLAR, FORMED . . . BY . . . JOHN TOWNELEY. Sale, 26 May, 1818, and following days. London, 1818.

The most important sale catalogue for the works of Hollar.

CATALOGUE OF A CHOICE COLLECTION OF THE WORKS OF WENCESLAUS HOLLAR, THE PROPERTY OF A DISTINGUISHED COLLECTOR. Sold by Mr. Evans. Feb. 9 and 10. London, 1821.

CATALOGUE OF THE . . . COLLECTION OF ENGRAVINGS BY WENCESLAUS HOLLAR AND WILLIAM FAITHORNE FORMED BY . . . LIEUT.-COLONEL DURRANT. Sale, 5 June, 1856. London, 1856.

PARTHEY, Gustav. Wenzel Hollar. Beschreibendes Verzeichniss seiner Kupferstiche. Berlin, 1853 (Nachträge und Verbesserungen. Berlin, 1858).

The standard catalogue of Hollar's works.

PARTHEY, Gustav. Kurzes Verzeichniss der Hollarschen, Kupferstiche. Berlin, 1853.

A complete list of Hollar's works without any of the detail of the descriptive catalogue.

BURLINGTON FINE ARTS CLUB. EXHIBITION OF A SELECTION FROM THE WORK OF WENCESLAUS HOLLAR. London, 1875. (The contributors to the exhibition were S. Addington, Sir F. Seymour Haden, Rev. J. J. Heywood, A. Morrison, and R. P. Roupell.)

BOROVSKY, F. A. Ergänzungen zu G. Parthey's Beschreibendem Verzeichniss seiner Kupferstiche. Prague, 1898.

A valuable supplement to Hollar's catalogue.

CATALOGUES OF EXHIBITIONS OF ETCHINGS BY WENCESLAUS HOLLAR. R. Gutekunst. London (10 Grafton St.), 1911 and 1913.

ARTICLES IN THE FOLLOWING DICTIONARIES:—

Bryan's *Dictionary of Painters and Engravers.*

Redgrave's *Dictionary of Artists of the English School.*

The Dictionary of National Biography.

Nagler's *Allgemeines Künstlerlexicon.*

BOOKS IN WHICH HOLLAR'S ETCHINGS
OF LONDON APPEARED

Reference is only given to locality of editions not in the General Library of the British Museum.

PRYNNE, William. Canterburies Doome. London (Printed by John Macock for Michael Spark Senior), 1646, fol.

See No. 88.

[VICARS, John]. A Sight of the Transactions of these latter yeares emblemized with engraven plats which men may read without spectacles. [London, 1646], (Sold by Thomas Jenner). Sm. 4°. Etched title page probably by Hollar (with allegorical figures of Time, Truth, and Envy).

See Nos. 24, 25, 31, 87, 93, 108.

[VICARS, John]. True Information of the Beginning and Cause of all our Troubles. London, 1648. Sm. 4°. B.M. Print Room.

See Nos. 24, 31, 87, 108.

[VICARS, John]. True Information of the Beginning, etc. London, " 1648 " [*i. e.* 1649 according to present calendar as Charles I's speech from the scaffold is given in a supplement]. Sm. 4°. B.M. Print Room, and Grenville, 4099.

See Nos. 24, 31, 108.

Ten of the small plates (each with two subjects) contained in the last three volumes cited are almost certainly by Hollar, though unsigned. They are precisely similar in style to Hollar's etchings of the *Trial and Execution of Strafford* of 1641, and the *Trial of Laud* of 1644 (see Nos. 91, 23 and 88). Hollar was already in Flanders by the date of the first publication, but his plates may quite well have been ready before his departure in 1644 or 1645. The latest event illustrated by the plates attributed entirely to Hollar is that of May 2, 1643 (*Destruction of Cheapside Cross;* see my No. 31). Only nine of the plates occur in the *Sight of the Transactions;* in the *True Information* several of the plates (each of which originally contained two subjects) being divided in half, and in some cases given a new title to fit an event of a later date. One plate (a single subject) occurring only in the second two volumes (at p. 27) shows part of the work in etching and part in coarse line-engraving. It is possibly a plate left unfinished by Hollar before he left England, and finished by the same poor engraver who did two other double plates which occur in all three books.

DODSWORTH, Roger, and DUGDALE, (Sir) William. Monasticon Anglicanum. London, fol.

Vol. I. 1655 (Printed by Richard Hodgkinson). See Nos. 99, 100.

Vol. II. 1661 (Printed by Alice Warren). See Nos. 21, 27.

Vol. III. (by William Dugdale alone), 1673 (Printed by Thomas Newcomb, and sold by A. Roper, J. Martin, and H. Herringham).

See Nos. 35, 36, 37, 39, 41, 119, 132.

There is a second edition of Vol. I., 1682, in the British Museum.

DUGDALE, (Sir) William. The Antiquities of Warwickshire. London (Printed by Thomas Warren. 1656, fol.).

2nd edition, continued by W. Thomas. 2 vols. London, 1730, fol.

3rd edition. 4 vols. Coventry, 1765, fol.

See No. 69.

KING, Daniel. The Cathedrall and Conventuall Churches of England and Wales orthographically delineated by D. K. Anno MDCLVI (engraved title). obl. fol.

A series of plates (without letterpress) used previously in Dodsworth and Dugdale, *Monasticon*, Vol. I. (1655), and later in the 2nd edition of the same (1682).

In the BRITISH MUSEUM LIBRARY copy (the only one known to me) there are 68 plates. Six are etched by Hollar, the rest by Daniel King. Drawings for a considerable number were supplied by Richard Newcourt, Thomas Johnson, Randall Holme, Stephen Anderton, and Richard Ralinson.

In this copy the plates occur in various states, before or with English title in addition to Latin, before or with numbers referring to pages of the *Monasticon*, and others with numbers which probably indicate a running numeration for King's series (more fully evidenced in the prints as they occur in B.M.L. copy of *Monasticon*, 2nd edition, 1682, with numbers which often do not tally with the pagination).

See Nos. 99 and 100.

HOWEL, James. Londinopolis. London, 1657, fol.

See No. 17.

DUGDALE, (Sir) William. The History of St. Paul's Cathedral. London (Printed by Thomas Warren), 1658, fol.

The pagination in this edition is curious. 136 is followed by 157–160. But it is more probably a mere printer's error than any indication of original intention of inserting the plates at this place.

2nd edition. London, 1716, fol. Some of the original plates are wanting, part of these being made up by copies engraved by John Harris. There are directions to the binder as to placing of certain plates which still bear old pagination.

See Nos. 32–67 (except No. 43).

OGILBY, John. The Entertainment of his most Excellent Majestie Charles II in his Passage through . . . London to his Coronation. London (T. Roycroft), 1662, fol

See No. 101.

SANCROFT, William. Lex Ignea, or the School of Righteousness. A sermon preach'd before the King, Octob. 10, 1666. At the Solemn Feast appointed for the late Fire in London. London (Printed for Timothy Garthwait), 1666. Sm. 4°.

[Later edition] (Printed for R. Pawlett), n.d. (but probably issued soon after the first edition, as Pawlett's activity is dated by Plomer, about 1660–1667). Sm. 4°.

See No. 68.

ASHMOLE, Elias. The Institution Laws and Ceremonies of the Most Noble Order of the Garter. London (Printed by J. Macock for Nathanael Brooke), 1672, fol. Second edition, 1693, fol.

See Nos. 114–118, 120–125, 127, 131.

BLOME, Richard. Britannia. London, 1673, fol.

See Nos. 8, 110.

OGILBY, John, and MORGAN, William. London Survey'd or, an Explanation of the Large Map of London. London. Published and sold at the Authors House in White-Fryers. 1677.

See No. 15.

SANDFORD, Francis. A Genealogical History of the Kings of England. London (Tho. Newcomb), 1677, fol.

2nd edition (continued by Samuel Stebbing). 1707, fol.

See Nos. 102–105, 128–130.

SPEED, John. Speed's Maps Epitomiz'd or the Maps of the Counties of England alphabetically placed. London, 1681, 8°. Includes 11 maps by Hollar (Map of England, Borovsky, 647a, and 10 County maps), others being engraved by R. Palmer. Of the County maps by Hollar, 5 are dated between 1667 and 1671 ; all bear dedications from the map draughtsman R. Blome, and some are also inscribed *London, printed for R. Blome.* Blome probably issued the maps separately 1667–1671, but there is no evidence of any volume before the present edition, nor of any states before the dedications belonging to edition of 1681.

See Nos. 1, 2, 3, and 111.

TAYLOR, Thomas. England exactly Described or a Guide to Travellers In a Compleat Sett of Mapps of all the County's of England. . . . Printed Coloured and Sold by Tho: Taylor at yᵉ Golden Lyon in Fleetstreet . . . [London, 1715].

There is no date on the title page, but the Map of the *North Part of Great Britain called Scotland* bears a dedication from Tho: Taylor dated 1715.

Contains the 10 County maps by Hollar which appeared earlier in *Speed's Maps Epitomiz'd,* 1681.

See Nos. 1, 2, 3, and 111.

[Later edition, with different title] England exactly Described . . . In a Compleat Sett of Maps of all the Counties of England . . . according to Mr. Ogilby's Survey. . . . Printed coloured and sold by Tho: Taylor at yᵉ Golden Lyon in Fleetstreet. . . . [London, 1716, or after].

Contains a map of Ireland with dedication from Tho: Taylor dated 1716.

Contains the 10 County maps by Hollar. See Nos. 1, 2, 3, and 111.

ASHMOLE, Elias. The Antiquities of Berkshire. London, 1719, 8°. 3 vols.

See No. 112.

CATALOGUE OF HOLLAR'S ETCHINGS OF LONDON AND WINDSOR

Dimensions, given in inches, are to the plate mark, except where otherwise described (as to border line, etc.). The first number refers to the height of the plate measured on the right side, the second to the breadth measured along the foot.

The locality of impressions is cited in the case of rare states. Where no reference to locality is given it may be assumed that an impression exists in the British Museum (which implies the Print Room, unless the Library is specified).

For the catalogue references (V. = Vertue, P. = Parthey, B. = Borovsky) see the list of *Chief Authorities consulted* (p. 26).

The arrangement is as follows :—

A (1–5)

COUNTY MAPS CONTAINING LONDON.

B (6–19)

MAPS, OR BIRD'S-EYE PLANS, AND GENERAL VIEWS OF LONDON

the Maps, or Plans, coming first, and the Views after ; with cross-references from the latter section to such views as occur in compartments on Maps.

C (20–108)

VIEWS OF SPECIAL PARTS AND BUILDINGS OF LONDON

starting from Greenwich, working westwards to the Tower, across the river to St. Mary Overy's (St. Saviour's, Southwark), back to the City, westward to St. Paul's, northwards to Islington, southwards and then westwards to Lincoln's Inn Fields, Covent Garden, Arundel House, Whitehall, Westminster, and Lambeth.

D (109–132)

RICHMOND AND WINDSOR.

A (1–5)

COUNTY MAPS CONTAINING LONDON

1. MAP OF ESSEX.

B. 661, b.—P. 671.

[6 × 8½]. Not signed, but certainly by Hollar. About 1667.
In compartment lower l., title and list : *Hundreds in Essex.*
II (?). Arms and dedication to Thomas Stringer.
in *Speed's Maps Epitomiz'd*, London, 1681 [No. 13 in the series, but before the number, in British Museum, King's Library copy].
III (?). Numbered *14* in upper r. Arms changed, and dedication to Josiah Child.
In T. Taylor, *England exactly Described* [London, 1715, and London, 1716?].

I have described the state in *Speed's Maps Epitomiz'd*, 1681, as provisional II, in order to be uniform with the *Map of Middlesex* (2), but I have not seen the conjectured earlier state. Compare also the *Map of Surrey* (3).

2. MAP OF MIDDLESEX.

P., B. 667.—V. III. 305 (and 316?).

[5¾ × 8⅜]. Signed and dated below towards l. : *W. Hollar fecit 1667.*
Title in compartment lower r. : *A Mapp of the County of Middlesex with its Hundreds by Rich: Blome. London Printed for Rich: Blome A⁰ 1667.*
I. Before dedication and arms. WINDSOR.
II. Arms and dedication to the Honble William Cheyne added in upper r.
In *Speed's Maps Epitomiz'd*, London, 1681 [No. 23 in the series, but before the number in B.M., King's Library copy].
III. Numbered *24* in upper r. Arms changed, and dedication to Sir Charles Gerard, Bart.
In T. Taylor, *England exactly Described* [London, 1715].
IV. *London Printed for Rich: Blome A⁰ 1677*, and words *Scale of miles* erased.
In T. Taylor, *England exactly Described* [London, 1716?].

3. MAP OF SURREY.

B. 668, a.—V. III. 319 (?).

[5¾ × 8⅜]. Signed in lower l. : *W: Hollar fecit.*
Title in compartment upper l. : *A Mapp of the County of Surrey.* At foot of Catalogue of the Hundreds : *London, Printed for Rich. Bloome A⁰ 1667.*

II (?). Arms and dedication to Sir Robert Clayton, Lord Mayor, 1680.
In *Speed's Maps Epitomiz'd*, London, 1681 [No. 34 in the series, but before the number in B.M., King's Library copy, in which it has been wrongly bound as 35].
III (?). Numbered *36* in upper r. Arms changed, and dedication to Sir Richard Onslow, Bart.
In T. Taylor, *England exactly Described* [London, 1715, and London, 1716 ?].

As this map was originally issued in 1667 (according to its inscription) there must have been an earlier state before the dedication to the Lord Mayor of 1680, with which it appeared in *Speed's Maps Epitomiz'd*, 1681, but I have not seen an impression.

4. MAP OF KENT.

P. 663.

[5½ × 8⅟₁₆]. Signed in lower l. margin : *W. Hollar fecit.*
The title in a rectangular compartment lower r. : *A Mapp of the County of Kent with its Lathes and Hundreds. By Rich: Blome, by his Maj^{ties} especiall Command.*
Along the lower margin eight rectangular compartments with names (the title, *The Table of Lathes and Hundreds*, being at top of compartment on the l.). WINDSOR.

This was probably issued by Blome about 1667–1670, but it was not used in *Speed's Maps Epitomiz'd*, 1681, or in T. Taylor, *England exactly Described* [London 1715, and 1716?], in which the map of Kent is a line-engraving and not by Hollar.

5. MAP OF KENT.

P. 664.

[12¼ × 15⅞]. Signed and dated in lower r. : *W. Hollar fecit 1670.*
Title in compartment lower r. : *A New Mapp of the County of Kent Dividea into the fives Lathes And subdivided into Hundreds.*
With a bird's-eye plan of Canterbury in compartment upper r.

B (6–19)

MAPS, OR BIRD'S-EYE PLANS, AND GENERAL
VIEWS OF LONDON

the Maps, or Plans, coming first, and the Views after ; with cross-references from the latter section to such views as occur in compartments on Maps.

6. BIRD'S-EYE PLAN OF THE WEST CENTRAL DISTRICT OF LONDON.

P., B. 1002.—Plate XIV.

[13⅝ × 18⅟₁₆] About 1658?.

The plan is similar in style and scale to P. 1006 (No. 12 below). It was probably intended to form a part of a larger plan, but there is no record of any other sheets going with it. It may have been part of the large map of London, unfinished in 1660,

D

to the expenses of which the King in that year requested the Aldermen and interested citizens to contribute.

Extent of the plan: W., to St. Martin's Lane; E., to Chancery Lane (northern part); N., beyond Holborn; S., the river from the Savoy to Essex Stairs.

The only known impression is in the British Museum. It has been reproduced by the London Topographical Society (1902), and there are notes on it in the Society's *London Topographical Record*, Vol. II. (1903), p. 109, by Mr. W. R. Lethaby, and Mr. Rhys Jenkins. In that place the map is dated by Mr. Lethaby as after the Fire, but Mr. Rhys Jenkins is more probably correct in placing it between the years 1656 and 1666. The latter bases his date on the presence of the obelisk-like tower called *Ye Waterhouse* standing in front of Arundel House, which was not put up until after 1655, and, as he argues, probably pulled down in 1665.[1] Moreover, the state of building in Lincoln's Inn Fields seems to point to a date about 1658 (see *L.C.C. Survey of London*, Vol. III. "Parish of St. Giles-in-the-Fields," edited by W. Edward Riley and Sir Laurence Gomme: London, 1912).

One of the reasons given by Mr. Lethaby for dating after the Fire is the assumed presence of the column and dial in the centre of Covent Garden, which was only erected in or just after 1668. I cannot, however, think that Hollar represents anything but a tree fenced-in in the centre of the Piazza. It is certainly not a column or dial. Hollar's view of Covent Garden (see No. 79 below), which was probably etched about 1640, shows no tree, but there is no reason why there should not have been an attempt to grow a tree in this position at some date between 1640 and 1668. The Piazza is surrounded by separate posts in the View (No. 79), but in the present Bird's-eye the posts are joined up to make a railing (or a new fence has been made) as shown in prints of the later seventeenth and eighteenth centuries.

The site of the Maypole (where St. Mary-le-Strand now stands) in the Strand is marked *At the Meypoo*. Maypoles were demolished at the time of the Commonwealth, and this one only seems to have been re-erected in 1661. It inclines one to suspect the print to be as late as 1661, but this would hardly agree with the condition of Lincoln's Inn Fields, and "The Maypole" may have remained the name for the place (at which hackney carriages stood) even during the absence of the Maypole itself. The following houses and palaces are marked on the plan: Salisbury House, Worcester House, Bedford House, Exeter House, the Savoy (see No. 84 for separate view of elevation from the river), Somerset House, and Arundel House (see Nos. 82 and 83).

It should be noted that the chief northern thoroughfare from E. to W. (High Holborn) curved south past St. Giles. The present straight road, New Oxford Street, was only constructed in 1847.

---

[1] Not to be confused with another similarly shaped waterhouse which stood near York Gate (near the present Charing Cross Underground station). This second waterhouse is not shown in Hollar's *Long View of London* of 1647 (No. 16 below), but appears in a drawing by Hollar in the Royal Library, Windsor. It shows the Thames looking towards the North Bank, with the Savoy. Somerset House, and Old St. Paul's in the distance.

7 (*a*). A MAP OF BOTH CITTIES LONDON AND WESTMINSTER, BEFORE THE FIRE.

P., B. 999.—V. III. 32.

[4⅛ × 7⅞ to border line ; 3¾ × 7¹³⁄₁₆ to inner border line of map alone without title].
Title as above in single line along the top. In corner spaces of the plan, letter and number references, starting upper l. : *A. The Citty of London*, and ending, r. : *36. Bishopsgate Strett.*

Borovsky describes a first state before the lettering, as in Windsor. But it cannot be found in the Royal Library, and Borovsky was probably in error.

Extent of map : E., to Wapping ; W., to part of Tothill Fields ; N., into clear country (as in P. 1005, No. 13, below) ; S., not entirely clear of the houses, *i. e.* less in extent than P. 1005.

This small bird's-eye plan occurs in the *Map of Great Britain and Ireland*, P. 648, V. III. 309.

[16⅜ × 20¾ to outer border line].
Title in cartouche in lower l. : *A New and Exact Map of Great Britannie. . . . London. Printed and published by John Overton at the White Horse without Newgate.*

Beside the Map of London here described, which is in a compartment in the upper r. corner, there are also plans of York, Edinburgh, Dublin, Oxford, Cambridge, and immediately below the Map of London, in upper r. :—

7 (*b*). PROSPECT OF THE CITTY OF LONDON AS IT APPEARED IN THE TIME OF ITS FLAMES.

[3⅛ × 7¹⁄₁₆ ; 2¾ × 7 to inner border line ; and compartment below with inscription : ¾ × 5⁹⁄₁₆].
The only inscription on the subject is *Southwarke* on the river near centre of print. On the compartment below the subject is the inscription in five lines : *On the 2 of September in yᵉ yeare 1666 (being the Lords day) in the morning, there hapned a dreadfull Fire, in yᵉ house of one Mʳ Farmer a Baker in pudding lane, which Continued till about 3 at night the Wednesday following, in which time it burnt 89 Churches thirteene thousand two hundred houses, 636 acres, of 97 Parishes within yᵉ Walls, there was but ii left intire, One Robert Hubert of Roame in Normandy, upon examination, confessed he was one that fired the first house (viz) Mʳ Farmers in Pudding lane, for which fact he was shortlie after hanged at Tiburne.*

Extent of view : E., beyond the Tower ; W., covering extent of Fire ; S., showing St. Mary Overy's complete as in P. 1005 (No. 13, below).

On the same Map as 7 (*a*). The Map itself is engraved, and not by Hollar, who is only responsible for the etched view and plans in the compartments.

8. BIRD'S-EYE PLAN OF LONDON BEFORE THE FIRE WITH THE ARMS OF THE CITY COMPANIES.

P., B. 1000.—V. III. 33.—Plate XI.

[6⅞ × 10⅞].

Title in centre above: *London.* Shows the arms of the City Companies at sides and along part of the lower border.

I. Before the arms of the City Companies. WINDSOR (the impression is cut, but as it shows $\frac{3}{16}$ inch outside inner border line of map, it is clear that the arms had not been engraved).

II. In lower margin, arms and dedication: *To the Hono^ble Sr Robert Vyner of the Citty of London Alderman, K^t and Baronet ; this Mapp is humbly dedicated by Ric: Blome.*

Occurs in R. Blome, *Britannia*, London, 1673, fol., at p. 149.

III. Address added beneath dedication: *Sold by S. Sympson Engraver Catherine Street Strand.* Not in British Museum or Windsor.

IV. *Before the Fire in 1666* added to the title *London.*

A French title takes the place of the dedication in margin: *Plan de Londres tel quil Etoi avant l'incendie de 1666. Gravé par Hollar.*

Extent of the map as in P. 1005 (No. 13): W., to Tothill Fields ; E., to Limehouse ; N., and S., clear of the town.

Sir Robert Vyner was elected alderman on 20th August 1666, but as he was sheriff for the year from June 1666, and this office is not mentioned in the dedication, the map probably dates after the end of his shrievalty, June 1667.

9. UNFINISHED BIRD'S-EYE PLAN OF PART OF THE CITY, BEFORE THE FIRE.

P. 1001.—V. III. 31.

[4$\frac{5}{16}$ × 6$\frac{11}{16}$]. Signed below towards l. (in I.): *W. Hollar.*

? I. Title above r.: *London.* The only other parts lettered are: *S. Paul, Cheape-side, Poultrie, Corn-hill, Lombard-streete, Leddenhall Streete, Broade Streete, Bishopsgate Streete, Gracechurch Streete, New Fisck Street.* BRITISH MUSEUM. WINDSOR.

? II. The title and signature erased. WINDSOR.

Extent of plan: W., covering upper part of Ludgate Hill ; E., to Aldgate ; S., to the Thames ; N., to London Wall.

Old St. Paul's is shown.

The corners of the plan upper r. and l., and lower r. are left blank, and more blank space also in lower l. than needed for river. It is probably an unfinished plate. The scale may be estimated thus: the length from beginning of Cornhill to Aldgate on the map is 3⅛ inches, *i. e.* the scale is rather larger than P. 1005 (No. 13).

The order of state is very puzzling, and the above is only what appears to me the more probable order, and not entirely convincing. Others whom I have consulted are about equally divided among those who accept and those who reverse the order given.

The title and signature on I. are etched or engraved over pieces of the plate, which has been scratched with the graver, as if for trying its point. They are not in a form in which they would be added on a finished state, but irregular marks and lettering such as would be cleared away when the plate was cleaned.

On the other hand, somewhat in favour of II. being the earlier state is the comparative strength of certain scratches, even though the general impression of the work is lighter and more delicate. Also the complete absence of any sign on the surface of II. of the work that has been burnished out.

The way in which the masts of vessels (without their hulls) are shown on the river bank, near the r., seems to point to a still earlier state in which the plate showed further work on the banks of the Thames, already burnished out in I.

10. PLAN OF LONDON AFTER THE FIRE, SHOWING THE PART DEMOLISHED.

P. 1003.—V. III. 29.

[9⅛ × 13¼]. Signed and dated in margin below l.: *W. Hollar fecit, 1666 : Cum privilegio Regis.*

Above in three lines the title: *A Map or Groundplott of the Citty of London with the Suburbes thereof so farr as the Lord Mayors Jurisdiction doeth extend by which is exactly demonstrated the present condition of it, since the last sade accident of fire, the blanke space signifÿng* (sic) *the burnt part, and where the houses be those places yet standing. A° 1666.*

Above r. in compartment: *Annotations of remarkable places.* Below l. in compartment: *The Names of all the Churches. . . .*

The plan is a bird's-eye in respect to the part of the city still standing.

Extent of the plan: W., covering part of Lincoln's Inn Fields; E., to the Tower; N., covering part of Bunhill and Finsbury Fields; S., covering part of Southwark.

This, the following two plans of the devastation caused by the Great Fire (No. 11), the parallel views of the city before and after event (No. 19), and the two views of the fire itself (in compartments on Nos. 7 and 12) tell their own tale. And the story of the Fire is too well known from Pepys's description to need repetition here. About five-sixths of the area of the city within the walls[1] was devastated by the fire. Only a few churches were left, the majority being rebuilt, and everything undertaken completed thirty years after the Fire. There was never a more remarkable opportunity for the architect, and the genius and energy of Sir Christopher Wren practically raised a new city within a generation. The houses may have lost their picturesqueness, but there is hardly a question that in the city of narrow streets the straighter fronts of late Jacobean architecture were more adapted to safety and utility. The greater loss was in the

---

[1] The walls of the old city extended round from Blackfriars to the Tower, but only the names of its gates (Ludgate, Newgate, Aldersgate, Cripplegate, Moorgate, Bishopsgate, and Aldgate), which were still standing in Hollar's time, are preserved to-day.

Gothic churches, where the question of utility need hardly be considered.   There was no attempt to rebuild on the old lines, practically everything being constructed in the Renaissance style, developed by Wren with wonderful genius and individuality, with something essentially English in his free treatment of classic architecture.   Both Sir Christopher Wren and the diarist Sir John Evelyn prepared plans for laying out the city in entirely new streets.   But while the Common Council were considering the scheme proposed, the people were at work on their old plots rebuilding with incredible rapidity.   London certainly lacks the vistas and harmonious combinations of squares, bridges and streets seen in so many foreign towns, but it is hardly a matter for regret that the schemes which might have built us on similar perfect lines was not carried into execution.   All the continuity of the history of the city would have thereby been lost, and much of the charm of the unexpected, which gives London its peculiar attraction amongst the great cities of the world.

11. ANOTHER PLAN OF LONDON AFTER THE FIRE, SHOWING THE PART DEMOLISHED.

P. 1004.—V. III. 28.

[$10\frac{3}{4} \times 13\frac{7}{8}$].   Signed and dated on lower margin of the compartment with small map : *W. Hollar fecit 1666.*

In compartment in upper r. the title : *A Map or Ground plot of the Citty of London, and the Suburbes thereof, that is to say, all which is witkin the Iurisdiction of the Lord Mayor or properlie calld't Londō by which is exactly demonstrated the present condition thereof, since the last sad accident of fire.   The blanke space signifeing* (sic) *the burnt part & where the houses are exprest, those places yet standīg.   Sould by John Overton at the White horse in little Brittaine, next doore to little S. Bartholomew Gate 1666.*

In compartment l. below another smaller bird's-eye plan with title in a small compartment in its upper r.: *A Generall Map of the whole Citty of London with Westminster & all the Suburbes by which may be computed the proportion of that which is burnt, with the other parts standing,* and letters of reference *a. Tuttle Fields* to *s. Charing Crosse.*

[$2\frac{15}{16} \times 16\frac{11}{16}$, to border line].

The extent of this small plan : E., to Limehouse, but otherwise nearly the same as the small map of London (No. 7, *a*) on the *Map of Great Britain and Ireland* (P. 648).

In the r. lower corner of main plan is a compartment with *Annotations of the Churches, and other remarkable places in this Map.*

I. Inscribed beneath the border line in lower margin l.: *Sould by Iokn Overton at the white horse neere the fountaine tavern without Newgate.* WINDSOR.

II. This inscription erased (but still showing the top of the *b* of *by,* which just crossed the border line beneath the first 6 of 1666 in signature).

The plan is a bird's-eye in respect to the part of the city still standing.

Extent of this main plan as in No. 10, to which it is otherwise very similar, only extending slightly further W., and showing more of Lincoln's Inn Fields.

There is a similar plan etched in Hollar's manner by Robert Pricke. Pricke followed the present map most nearly, but he probably also used No. 10.

[About 16⅝ × 19⅞].

Title above in two lines : *An Exact map representing the condition of the late famous .. . City of London as it lyeth in its ruins. . . .*

To the r. below : *Are to be sould by Robert Pricke in Whitecrosse street neare Cripplegate Church.*

The small map of London in centre below (signed : *R. P. fecit et excudit*), and on either side of this small map : (l.) *the Names of all the Churches*, (r.) *the names of the Halls . . . and other places of note*. BRITISH MUSEUM, CRACE COLLECTION, and KING'S LIBRARY, K. 20. 18.

A SMALL PLAN OF LONDON AFTER THE FIRE, SHOWING THE PART DEMOLISHED.

Forms part of the *Plan of London after the Fire showing the part demolished*, No. 11, *q. v.*

12. AN EXACT SURVEIGH OF THE STREETS CONTAINED WITHIN THE RUINS OF THE CITY OF LONDON (BY JOHN LEAKE). 1669.

P. 1006.—V. III. 40.—Plates XII. and XIII.

On two plates.

(*a*) Left portion [21¾ × 16⅝] ; (*b*) right portion [21¾ × 16½].

Signed in lower r. of (*b*) *Wenceslaus Hollar fecit 1667.*

The title above running across (*a*) and (*b*) : *An exact Surveigh of the Streets Lanes and Churches contained within the ruines of the City of London first described in six plats by John Leake, John Jennings, William Marr, Willm Leybourn, Thomas Streete, and Richard Shortgrave in Dec:^ber A° 1666 . . . reduced here into one intire plat by John Leake. . . .*

(*a*) Contains in an oblong compartment above a view with the title on a scroll along the top : *The Prospect of this Citty as it appeared from the opposite Southwarke side, in the fire time* [4⅞ × 16¼, to border line].

In lower l. of (*a*) *Published . . . by . . . Nathanaell Brooke Stationer, and are to be sould at his shop at the Angell in the second Yard of Gresham Colledge leading from Bishopsgate street.*

(*b*) Compartment in upper r. with numbers and letters of reference to churches, halls, etc.

In upper l. compartment with inscription *The Right Honourable Sr William Turner the Lord Major* (sic) *A° 1669.*

The inscription to the Lord Mayor no doubt gives the date of first publication, though Hollar's work was apparently done in 1667.

Extent of plan (which is a bird's-eye in respect to part of the city still standing) : N., covering part of Bunhill and Finsbury Fields ; S., part of Southwark ; W., to Essex House and Holborn Bar (rather less W. than P. 1003 and 1004, *i. e.* Nos. 10 and 11, not including Lincoln's Inn Fields) ; E., the Tower (as in Nos. 10 and 11). In l. portion the plan is cut off just above Hatton Garden by the *Prospect.*

Extent of the *Prospect* in compartment : E., London Bridge ; W., to Fleet Ditch.

This *Exact Surveigh* has been reproduced in facsimile by the London Topographical Society (1908 and 1909). The only impressions to which I can refer are in the BRITISH MUSEUM (CRACE COLLECTION), PEPYS LIBRARY (MAGDALENE COLLEGE, CAMBRIDGE), and WINDSOR. The larger scale map referred to in the title above as *first described in six plats by John Leake* (and others) . . . *in Dec:ᵇᵉʳ Aᵒ 1666* remains a mystery. As this survey, the first after the Fire, was made for the Corporation, one would expect to find a copy, if it exists, in the Guildhall Library. But Mr. Kettle, the Librarian to the Corporation, who has been troubled by the same question, has found no trace of it, and, in spite of the date of publication being so definitely cited on the present map, thinks that the original larger survey may never have got beyond manuscript. There would in any case have been surprisingly little time between the Fire in September and December 1666, for a survey to have been made, engraved, and published.

18. A NEW MAP OF THE CITTIES OF LONDON, WESTMINSTER AND YE BOROUGH OF SOUTHWARKE

P. 1005.—V. III. 30.

[17¾ × 23⅝]. Signed and dated in lower r. : *W: Hollar fecit, 1675.*
The main title occurs in a decorated cartouche towards upper r. of main plan :
A new map of the citties of London, Westminster, and ye borough of Southwarke with their Suburbs shewing yᵉ streets, lanes, allies, Courts, etc. . . . as they are now truly and carefully delineated. Sold by Robert Green at ye Rose & Crown, in Budg-Row. And by Robert Morden, at ye Atlas in Cornhill, London.
In a strip above the main plan is a view of London with title on scroll above :—
Prospect of London as it was flourishing before the destruction by fire.
[4¹⁄₁₆ × 23¼, to border line].

The map is a bird's-eye of great minuteness.

Extent of plan (similar to P. 1000, No. 8 above) : W., to Lambeth and part of Tothill Fields ; E., to Limehouse ; N., and S., into clear country.

The *Prospect* on strip above is excellent. The point of view is rather further south than the Large View of 1647, as it shows S. Mary Overy's complete. It also shows generally more of the S. of the Thames, giving a very attractive view of the gardens to the houses. Its extent E. is about the same as the Large View of 1647, but W. it only extends to Worcester House (just W. of the Savoy).

The Towneley Catalogue (No. 93) dates the map 1677, probably in error. There is no dedication to lead one to place its publication two years after Hollar signed the work (as in P. 1006, No. 12 above).

14. OGILBY AND MORGAN'S LARGE MAP OF LONDON. 1677.

P., B. 1007.—V. III. 38.

The map printed from twenty plates; an extra plate containing decorative borders, etc. There must have also been another plate with further marginal numbers.

TITLE IN TYPE

(Dedication)

	1	2	3	4	5	6	7	8	9	10	11	12	13	14	15	16	17	18	19	20	
1 — 2	I				II				III				IV				V				1 — 2
3 — 4 — 5	VI				VII				VIII				IX				X				3 — 4 — 5
6 — 7 — 8	XI				XII				XIII				XIV				XV				6 — 7 — 8
9 — 10 — 11	XVI				XVII				XVIII				XIX				XX				9 — 10 — 11
	1	2	3	4	5	6	7	8	9	10	11	12	13	14	15	16	17	18	19	20	

Impressions from the twenty plates when pieced together come in four rows, each containing five pieces, as in our sketch I–XX. Each of these plates had an Arabic numeral in its margin corresponding to its place, to help the printer, but in piecing together, the small margin is generally cut off so that the number is not usually visible. Not counting the small blank margin, the plates of top row measure about $9\frac{7}{8} \times 20$; those of the second and third rows about $15\frac{3}{4} \times 20$; the lowest row about $14\frac{7}{8} \times 20$. The map is divided for convenience of reference into 20 perpendicular, and 11 horizontal strips (of about 5 inches broad), and in a complete impression the numbers 1–20 would come along top and bottom, and the numbers 1–11 on either side. Of these numbers those at the side are from engraved plates, those at the top and bottom from type (except Nos. 10 and 11 in the centre of the top, which were engraved immediately beneath the dedication to Charles II on another plate).

The main title is printed in type and mounted along the top: *A Large and Accurate Map of the City of London Ichnographically Describing all the Streets, Lanes,*

Alleys, Courts, Yards, Churches, Halls and Houses, &c. Actually Surveyed and Delineated. By John Ogilby Esq ; His Majesties Cosmographer.

The Dedication to Charles II comes in a decorative cartouche in the centre of the upper margin immediately above Nos. 10 and 11. It is inscribed *To the High and Mighty Monarch Charles the II. . . . London actually survey'd by John Ogilby Esq and Wm Morgan is most humbly dedicated by . . . William Morgan.*

In the upper left corner of piece I of the map the City arms, and in a cartouche the inscription : *To the Right Hon:^rble ye Ld Major Court of Aldermen and Sheriffs of the Honble City of London this most accurate Survey . . . is dedicated and presented by . . . Witł Morgan his Ma^tys Cosmograph^r* [the last few lines showing that the inscription had been altered on the plate before any of the known impressions].

In the upper r. corner of piece V is a coat of arms (*Sable a fess between 3 ducks argent*), and beneath it an empty cartouche. The coat is that of Sir Joseph Sheldon (Lord Mayor 1675–76), which shows that the map was at least started, if not finished, in the year before the publication of the text.

Belonging to the plan is a twenty-first engraved plate of about the same size as the other pieces [14⅞ × 20⅛], containing various pieces of decoration : *i. e.* (*a*) the cartouche with dedication to Charles II and Nos. 10 and 11 beneath [about 3⅛ × 8⅛], (*b*) a long strip of border decoration, with two grotesque heads and four wreaths [about 1 × 16½], (*c*) a broader strip of scroll decoration with female bust in centre and peacocks at side [3¾ × 16½], (*d*) another strip of scroll decoration with Charles II's monogram surmounted by crown and supported by Lion and Unicorn in centre [3¾ × 16½], (*e*) six narrow border pieces with the Nos. 1, 2, 3, 4, 5, 6 (each in division of about 5 inches, to be cut up and used as references at side of map), (*f*) a narrow strip for upright border decoration, with a female figure on pedestal and bearing basket of flowers on her head [1 × 6¾], (*g*) an inscription, *The Atcheivment of the Honble City of London* [2½ × 4¼], (*h*) a long strip showing the river with six boats [2 × 19¾], (*i*) a small piece showing four and a half of the piers of London Bridge with the swirl of water, and a boat [2 × 2⅞].

Of this plate (*h*) and (*i*) alone are etched, and by Hollar. The other parts are engraved, and almost certainly by another hand, a heraldic engraver.

The only impressions I have examined are :—

GUILDHALL LIBRARY. The twenty plates complete, and separate ; also the additional decorative plate (only known to me in this collection).

BRITISH MUSEUM, Print Room. Two complete impressions of the map.

(*a*) Published 1857. Mounted with reference numbers as described above and indicated in our sketch ; also showing the bottom of the cartouche (from the additional plate) containing dedication to Charles II with the Nos. 10 and 11 beneath : the upper part has been cut off. Without the main title along top, or other decoration.

(*b*) Crace collection. Mounted on a roller. Wanting the main title along top (which has been put in in pen and ink) ; also wanting the reference numbers at top and sides. Does not show dedication to Charles II, or any of the other decorations.

[There are also separate pieces of an incomplete set in the Crace collection.]

BRITISH MUSEUM LIBRARY. Maps, S. 12 (27). With title above, but without the reference numbers at side. Cut into 56 pieces and mounted on canvas. With no further decoration.

WINDSOR, Royal Library. Incomplete; without title above, and only 15 pieces of the map.

The Print Room impression (*a*) is the only one in which I have found elements used printed from the plate of decoration only represented in the Guildhall. The other engraved numbers at the side (7–11) connote the existence of at least one further copper plate. The strips of decoration were undoubtedly intended for the border (cf. *e.g.*, Ogilby and Morgan's map of 1682),[1] but the only part from the Guildhall additional plate whose intended position is proved is the dedication to Charles II. Two parts which would seem to have no place as decoration are the etched pieces of the river and London Bridge, which closely resemble parts of the etched plan. Considering these two pieces alone one might be inclined to accept Mr. Charles Welch's view that the additional plate was a sort of specimen plate for a prospectus of the map. But as this theory cannot hold good for the engraved decoration, I should prefer to regard the aim of the etched pieces as still unsolved.

The inscription, *The Atcheivment . . . of London*, has a light border line which would exactly fit into the empty cartouche in the right-hand upper corner of piece V of the plan. Whether this space was intended to receive it, or some personal dedication indicated by the arms above, I cannot say.

The map is not signed by Hollar, and he is certainly not responsible for the whole work. But parts of the plan are probably his, *e.g.*, the river, its boats, and the tower (with the lettering in Hollar's characteristic style), the trees in the Temple Gardens and possibly Gray's Inn (but scarcely those in Moorfields and Charterhouse). The figures in the New Artillery Gardens are hardly good enough for Hollar. The general plan itself might be also by Hollar, but I think it doubtful whether he was responsible for much. He certainly did not do the engraved arms and cartouches in the upper corners.

Extent of map: E., covering the Tower; W., half of Lincoln's Inn Fields; N., Bunhill Fields; S., the river; scale: 100 ft. to an inch.

Ogilby and Morgan published a small volume of explanatory text to the map. The only copy known is in the British Museum. It is entitled *London Survey'd or, an Explanation of the Large Map of London . . . by John Ogilby and William Morgan. London. Published and sold at the Authors House in White-Fryers.* 1677. The frontispiece is a small bird's-eye plan, described below (No. 15). The dedication of the volume is to the Lord Mayor, Sir Thomas Davis. Beside the title and dedication, there are ten unnumbered pages of introductory matter, and forty-eight numbered pages with lists of streets, etc., and references to the map.

---

[1] This map is generally erroneously named Morden and Lea's Map after the publishers who re-issued it in 1732. It has been reproduced by the London Topographical Society, and described by Mr. Walter L. Spiers, *London Topographical Record*, V. (1908), p. 117.

Both map and volume of text were reproduced in facsimile by the London and Middlesex Archeological Society, 1895, the text with introduction by Charles Welch. A reduced reproduction of the map is given in Sir Walter Besant's *London in the Time of the Stuarts*, 1903.

15. A SMALL PLAN OF LONDON AFTER THE FIRE.

P. 999, a (Nachträge).—V. III. 26.

[3½ × 6⅜]. Signed lower l.: *W. Hollar* (visible in Coburg impression ; the W. H. being in monogram). [1677.]

The title in centre above : *London.*

I. Before the Pair of Compasses, the Scale of Miles, and the Mariner's Compass. Also before several of the other inscriptions. *To Hamsted* in wrong place. WINDSOR (cut impression).

II. Below r., a Pair of Compasses marking the Scale (*one mile in an inch*). In centre below, the dial of a Mariner's Compass.

Various inscriptions added : *To Tatnum Court* where *To Hamsted* occurred in I., and *To Hampsted* added in correct place. WINDSOR. BRITISH MUSEUM. COBURG. PEPYS LIBRARY (MAGDALENE COLLEGE, CAMBRIDGE).

Extent of the map which is a minute bird's-eye : beyond the town in every direction, the most extensive of all Hollar's plans (rather further E. and W. than No. 8). W., well beyond St. James's Park and Tothill Fields ; E., to the Isle of Dogs.

Parthey only describes it from a separate impression in Coburg. I find that it is the frontispiece to John Ogilby and William Morgan, *London Survey'd, or an Explanation of the Large Map of London*, 1677 (unique copy in the British Museum, see notes to No. 14). The signature is not visible on the Museum impression. At either end of the map (placed sideways in the British Museum book) is title in type : (left, *i. e.* above as it occurs in book), *Map of London, Westminster, and Southwark :* (right, *i. e.* below, in book), *At one Mile in an Inch.*

16. LONG BIRD'S-EYE VIEW OF LONDON FROM BANKSIDE. 1647.

P. 1014.—V. III. 1.—Plates XV–XX and XX, A.

On six plates, each about 18¾ × 15½ in. One of the six plates contains the two end-pieces of the view, so that the map would be composed of seven sheets when put together in order. The sheets may be referred to as 1–7 from l. to r., No. 7 being the r. end-piece.

The title, LONDON, in a cartouche above in centre of Sheet 4. On Sheet 1 (l. end-piece): sixteen Latin verses (in two columns) with title *Ad Londinum Epitomen & Ocellum ;* below this a dedication to Princess Mary of Orange, *Serenissimae Mariae . . . hunc amœnissimum celeberrimi Londinensis emporij ac sedes regalis aspectum. D. C. Q. Cornelius Danckers,* and the signature *Wenceslaus Hollar delineavit, et fecit*

Londini et Antverpiæ, 1647. At the foot a small VIEW OF WESTMINSTER AND TOTHILL FIELDS FROM THE SOUTH OF THE RIVER [$1\frac{3}{4} \times 7\frac{9}{16}$, to inner border line], showing reference numbers to 1. *Parlement house* | 2. *Westminster Hall* | 3. *Westminster Abby* | 4. *the Cloke house.* This small view is an extension (marked by a *) from the extreme left of the large view to beyond Tothill Fields.

On Sheet 7 (r. end-piece): thirty-four Latin verses (in two columns) with title *De Celeberrima & Florentissima Trinobantiados Augustae Civitate,* signed *Edw. Benlowes Armiger;* and below the publisher's address, *Prostant Amstelodami apud Cornelium Danckers in via Vitulina sub insigni Gratitudines An⁰. 1647.*

State I. BRITISH MUSEUM. GUILDHALL. WINDSOR.

State II. Shows the following changes: on Sheet 3, the Tower of St. Paul's is altered to a dome, with a flag flying at top, and *S. Pauwls Church* now reads *S. Pauwls Cathedrall;* on Sheet 4, the *Monument* is added, between the two church towers furthest r.

WINDSOR (imperfect, wanting the two end-pieces, so that I cannot refer to any changes, if any were made, in the inscriptions). The plate is printed darker in this state, and has probably been rebitten. The dome of St. Paul's is not in the form as it was completed, so that the plate in this state may have been issued before the building was finished (*i. e.* before 1697). But it probably dates after the completion of the Monument (which was in building between 1671–1677).

There is an early copy by Robert Pricke, which has sometimes (*e. g.* in the Towneley Catalogue, 86) been described as a late state of the original. It is on six plates, each measuring about $19\frac{1}{2} \times 15$ in. The title along the lower margin in large capitals: *The Exact Representation of the South Prospect of the Famous Citie of London being the Metropolitan of Great Britain. Robert Pricke Excud.*

In a compartment on the l. end-piece, where the text stood in the original, is the *Judgment of Solomon;* in another compartment, on the r. end-piece, is a *View of the Port,* and the signature *R. Pricke fecit et excudit.* BRITISH MUSEUM (KING'S LIBRARY). WINDSOR (only the end-pieces). This copy is dated 1664 in the British Museum Library catalogue, but I do not know on what grounds. In any case, it is probably before the Fire, or at least before the rebuilding, as no changes are made in the view itself.

Extent of view: W., to half-way between Whitehall and Westminster Abbey (the small view at foot of l. end-piece continues W. to include Tothill Fields); E., to beyond St. Katherine's. The view might have been taken from the tower of St. Mary Overy's (which does not appear), or some high point near by. A large extent of fields and gardens on the south side of the river is shown W. of Winchester House. A photogravure facsimile has been published by the London Topographical Society. A reduced reproduction was issued by the Art for Schools Association.

According to Hollar's signature this view was etched in Antwerp in 1647. But it was no doubt based on drawings made by the artist while in London between 1637 and 1644. He probably also used Visscher's etched view of 1616 as an aid. Both

Visscher's and Hollar's views are generally regarded as faithful records of the general appearance of the city, but constant differences (in the form of towers, etc.), more than can be accounted for by the difference of date, warn us against taking either as accurate representations of architectural detail. London before the Fire was almost entirely composed of Gothic buildings, Inigo Jones's Banqueting Hall at Whitehall, and the portico and classical restorations at St. Paul's being among the few pieces of Renaissance architecture that appear in Hollar's print. The finest houses of the great nobility, as well as the Royal Palace of Whitehall, are almost all along the north bank of the river between Westminster and Blackfriars. The chief of these marked on the view (from W. to E.) are Suffolk House (later known as Northumberland House, and taken down as recently as 1874 to make place for Northumberland Avenue), York House (given by Queen Mary to Heath, Archbishop of York, according to Stow "in recompense for York House, Whitehall,[1] which her father, Henry VIII, had taken from Cardinal Wolsey and from the see of York"; it later belonged to Sir Francis Bacon, and to George Villiers Duke of Buckingham, who erected a new house, of which the water-gate, said to have been designed by Inigo Jones, at the bottom of Buckingham Street, on the embankment is the only relic), Durham House (before the Reformation, belonging to the see of Durham; later inhabited by Sir Walter Ralegh, Lord Keeper Coventry, Philip Herbert, Earl of Pembroke, etc.), Salisbury House, the Savoy (see No. 84), Somerset House (an earlier building than the present house, which was built 1776–1786; it originally belonged to the Protector Somerset, and became the property of the Crown on his attainder; Henrietta Maria, and Catherine of Braganza resided here), Arundel House (see Nos. 82 and 83), Essex House, Baynard's Castle (built in 1428 by Humphrey, Duke of Gloucester; forms the background of a famous scene in Shakespeare's Richard III; according to Evelyn it was garrisoned by the Parliament in 1648; destroyed in the Fire).

The "New Exchange" (a popular shopping resort from the time of the Restoration till the end of Queen Anne's reign) is said to have been built in 1608–1609 on the site of part of Durham House, but it is marked on the view (perhaps in error) E. of Salisbury House. The mouth of the River Fleet (or rather Fleet "ditch") is shown opposite the Globe Theatre. Since the making of Blackfriars Bridge in 1765 the Fleet has been covered in, but the mouth of its underground conduit may still be seen beneath Blackfriars Bridge. The Globe Theatre shown in the view is not Shakespeare's theatre, though it was built before his death. The earlier Globe (of which there is a small view on the map of the British Isles in John Speed's "Theatre of the Empire of Great Britaine," 1611) was burnt down in 1613, but almost immediately rebuilt. A similar building near the Globe recalls the Elizabethan sport of bear-baiting, which retained its popularity long after Pepys's time. For the Swan Theatre, not shown on this view, see the "Londinopolis" view, No. 17.

The eel ships (Sheet 3) shown immediately opposite Winchester House (which was not used as an episcopal house after 1626, though it remained in existence until a fire

---

[1] See note to Whitehall (No. 85).

in 1814), may still be seen stationed just below London Bridge. They are moored in the Thames to represent the chartered rights of Dutch fishermen to sell eels in Billingsgate. Another record of foreign commerce is the Steel-yard (*Stiliard*) on the river immediately south of Bow Church. It was originally the house of foreign merchants of the Hanseatic League. The Hanse merchants were banished by Elizabeth in 1597–1598 (and the Steel-yard itself used as a storehouse for the Navy), but they were allowed to return by James I in 1606. This remarkable foreign commercial house remained in existence until 1853, having been long in the hands of the Jacobsen and Colquhoun families. The house (as rebuilt after the Fire) was pulled down in 1863 to make way for Cannon Street Railway Station.

St. Mary Overy's (St. Saviour's, Southwark) is just out of the view, being possibly the point from which the whole was taken. The richly decorated buildings in the centre of old London Bridge (Sheet 5) which forms a delightful piece in this view, is old Nonsuch House. The close arches of the Bridge, which formed a barrier to floating ice during cold winters, explains to some extent why so much is heard of frost fairs in the Thames in the seventeenth and eighteenth centuries. It should be noted that New London Bridge (opened in 1831) is placed 180 feet west of the old structure, robbing the Monument of its natural place at the entrance to the Bridge. There are as yet no docks, the river itself being London's haven (see note under No. 21). The Tower of the old Royal Exchange (see Nos. 28 and 29) forms almost the centre of the whole view beneath the title (Sheet 4).

Old St. Paul's is seen without the spire, which was struck by lightning and destroyed by fire in 1561. No restoration was taken in hand beyond a temporary lead roof.

Hollar's imperfect mastery of English may be remarked in the spelling of many of the titles on the buildings, e.g. *S. Pauwls*, *Boo Church*, and *S. Lorentz*.

17. "THE LONDINOPOLIS" VIEW OF LONDON.

P., B. 1012.—V. III. 34.—Plate XXI.

[$9\frac{3}{8} \times 12\frac{1}{2}$, plate line; $7\frac{3}{8} \times 12\frac{3}{8}$, border line of subject].

The title, LONDON, with two verses, *London the glory of Great Britaines Ile | Behold her Landschip here, and tru pourfile*, in cartouche above in centre.

In the margin below references to the map numbered 1–46.

Extent of the map: W., to Whitehall (part); E., to St. Katherine's. The view includes St. Mary Overy's, and is taken on that account from a point further south than the *Long View* of 1647. But the point of view is lower than in the view of 1647, and consequently shows less of the open land S. of the river W. of the Globe Theatre. The Swan Theatre (not shown in the *Long View* of 1647) appears in this view. It occurs also in Visscher's view of London of 1616. Mr. H. B. Wheatley (*London Past and Present*, 1891) states that it appears to have been swept away about 1633. The present view would seem to negative that hypothesis, but its absence in the view of 1647 is puzzling, unless it was cleared away before 1647 and rebuilt during the next years.

Occurs folded facing p. 1 of James Howel, *Londinopolis:* London, 1657.

There is a close copy (it follows the original in detail, but is throughout harder in line; the original shows a slipped stroke across the lower part of the arms of the City; the white spaces of this coat of arms are quite clear of any scratches in the copy).

There is a second copy (WINDSOR) in which the view is given on a narrower plate [2⅝ × 12, to border line]. It bears the title *A Prospect of London as before the Fire* on a narrow scroll above. It was wrongly described by Borovsky as a later state of the original.

THE PROSPECT OF THIS CITTY AS IT APPEARED FROM THE OPPOSITE SOUTHWARKE SIDE IN THE FIRE TIME.

Occurs in a compartment on the left portion (*a*) of *An Exact Surveigh* (by John Leake), published 1669, described under No. 12, above, *q. v.*

PROSPECT OF LONDON AS IT WAS FLOURISHING BEFORE THE DESTRUCTION BY FIRE.

Occurs in a compartment along the top of the *New Map of the Citties of London, Westminster, and ye borough of Southwarke,* described under No. 13, above, *q.v.*

PROSPECT OF THE CITTY OF LONDON AS IT APPEARED IN THE TIME OF ITS FLAMES.

Occurs in a compartment on the *Map of Great Britain and Ireland,* P. 648, and described as No. 7 (*b*), above, *q. v.*

18. THE PROSPECT OF LONDON AND WESTMINSTER TAKEN FROM LAMBETH.

P. 1013.—V. III. 36.—Plates XXII–XXV.

On four plates, each about 12¾ × 15 in.

Title as above, followed by the words *by W: Hollar,* in cartouche in centre of upper margin (divided between Sheets 2 and 3). Two lines of inscriptions below with reference numbers (1–40) and letters (*a*—*az*) to places.

The view is taken from nearly above and behind Lambeth Palace. The river scarcely seen E. of Somerset House. Extent W., to Peterborough House (*i. e.* just short of Tothill Fields, which are included in the *Long View* of 1647).

Of particular interest as showing the fields on the S. side of the Thames.

BRITISH MUSEUM, PRINT ROOM AND LIBRARY (three impressions). WINDSOR. GUILDHALL.

This view is described by Parthey as *London before the Fire,* but I have only seen impressions showing the new St. Paul's Cathedral. These impressions all show what seems to be rework (coarsely done, and hardly by Hollar) on Sheets 3 and 4, and the town as rebuilt on the parts destroyed by the Fire. St. Paul's shows its dome, but only one of the W. towers. The Monument is shown, and a reference to it (*at*) at the foot of Sheet 4. It may be taken as dating after the completion of the Monument (which was in building 1671–1677). It is dated 1674 in the Crace collection catalogue, but I do not know on what foundation.

The two left sheets (1 and 2) show Hollar's work most purely. Unless Hollar left the other plates unfinished, one must expect to find impressions of the earlier state before the coarser rework. The plates of this subject descended to the eighteenth-century printseller Robert Sayer, and no doubt after him to his successors, Laurie and Whittle (cf. No. 19), so that late and reworked impressions are common, It was published in this late state with the impressions from each plate folded for binding.

19. PARALLEL VIEWS OF LONDON BEFORE AND AFTER THE FIRE.
P., B. 1015.—V. III. 35.—Plates XXVI and XXVII.

On two plates: (*a*) left portion, $8\frac{7}{8} \times 13\frac{3}{8}$; (*b*) right portion, $8\frac{7}{8} \times 13\frac{5}{8}$. Signed and dated in lower r. margin: *Wenceslaus Hollar delin: et sculp. 1666*, the title LON|DON above in centre, half on each plate. Along the top of the upper view (across the two plates) the sub-title: *A True and Exact Prospect of the famous City of London from S. Marie Overs | Steeple in Southwarke in its Flourishing Condition before the Fire. designed by W: Hollar of Prage, Boh:ᵉⁿ*.

Along the top of the lower view (across the two plates) the second sub-title: *Another prospect of the sayd Citty taken from the same place as it | appeareth now after the sad Calamitie and Destruction by Fire, In the Yeare* M.DC.LXVI.

In a long compartment at the foot numbers (1–58) with references to buildings in the views.

I. Before Overton's address. [I have not seen an impression in this state.]

II. Address added in lower l. margin of left-hand plate: *Sould by John Overton at the White Horse in little Brittaine, next doore to little S. Bartholomewes gate.* BRITISH MUSEUM (KING'S LIBRARY).

III. Address now reads: *Sould—White Horse* (as before) *at the corner of the little old Baly neere the fountaine tavern without Newgate.* BRITISH MUSEUM. WINDSOR.

IV. *Cum privilegio* added after Hollar's signature. WINDSOR.

V. Overton's address erased. *Published by Laurie and Whittle,* 53 *Fleet Street, London, | Successor to the late Mʳ Robert Sayer* added in centre of lower margin (part on each plate).

VI. The address in the centre as well as Overton's address now erased. Coarsely rebitten. GUILDHALL.

Extent of the views: from the Temple to the Tower.

E

For a short note on the Great Fire, see No. 10. The number of towers still standing after the Fire is noteworthy, but the majority of the churches were so gutted that they had to be pulled down and entirely rebuilt. It is remarkable that practically the whole of the outer walls of the Cathedral are standing. See Philip Norman in the *London Topographical Record* (London Topographical Society), Vol. V. (1908), p. 26, for "London City Churches that escaped the Great Fire."

(C 20–108)

VIEWS OF SPECIAL PARTS AND BUILDINGS OF LONDON

starting from Greenwich and working westwards to the Tower, across the river to St. Mary Overy's (St. Saviour's, Southwark), back to the City, westward to St. Paul's, northwards to Islington, southwards and then westwards to Lincoln's Inn Fields, Covent Garden, Arundel House, Whitehall, Westminster, and Lambeth.

20. GREENWICH.

P., B. 977.—V. III. 21.—Plates XXVIII and XXIX.

[On two plates: (*a*) left half, 6 × 16$\frac{9}{16}$; (*b*) right half, 6 × 16$\frac{5}{8}$]. The title *Graen|wich* in the centre of sky above, half on each plate.

I. The cartouche l. contains the following dedication to the Queen Henrietta Maria: *Serenissimae Potentissimae | et Excel:^{mae} Principissae Henriettae Mariae | . . . hanc Grenovicensis tractus Tabellam manu sua delineatam, Wenceslaus Hollar Bohē: Excellentissimi Arundelliae et Surriae Comitis Caelator, humillime dedicat consecratque Anno 1637.*

With heavy clouds in the sky, chiefly on the right half. Inscribed *London* over the distant city (left half of plate).

BRITISH MUSEUM. (The impression mentioned by Parthey [Nachträge] as purchased by Colnaghi was acquired for the British Museum in 1855.) WINDSOR. (Possibly the impression exhibited at the Burlington Club Exhibition by Rev. J. J. Heywood.)

II. The dedication to Henrietta Maria erased, and the cartouche white. BRITISH MUSEUM. PRAGUE. PEPYS LIBRARY (MAGDALENE COLLEGE, CAMBRIDGE).

III. On the cartouche: four verses *Ad ripas—per orbem* (signed) *Hen: Peachamus*, and beneath verses the signature: *W: Hollar, Bohem, delin: Anno 1637.* The heavy clouds cleared from the sky. WINDSOR.

IV. Four English verses added where the signature stood in III.: *Behould, by Prospect, with what art | Fayre Greenwich Castle, pleasantly | A House of Banquet, neare & part | Of Thames, and London, how they ly.* New signature, *W. Hollar fecit*, added on lower scroll of cartouche. Below l. in margin: *London Printed and sould by Peter Stent at the Crowne in Gilt spur street betwixt new Gate and pie Corner.* BRITISH MUSEUM. WINDSOR.

The house on the hill in the left foreground, rebuilt in the time of Henry VIII on the site of an ancient tower or castle, was again rebuilt in 1675 and used as an observatory by John Flamsteed, the first Astronomer Royal, and called Flamsteed House. The present observatory occupies the same site.

The large house at the foot of the park to the right of (*a*) appears to be the "Queen's House," begun in the time of James I, and said to have been finished by Inigo Jones in 1635 for Henrietta Maria (I quote from a note kindly given me by Mr. Philip Norman).

The earliest dated London view. The removal of the dedication to the Queen is a sign of the times. Hollar was a Royalist, but he no doubt feared at a time when the Court was unpopular that the dedication might prejudice the sale of his print.

21. ST. KATHERINE'S BY THE TOWER.

P. 1032.—V. IX. 223.—Plate XXX.

[$7\frac{5}{16} \times 11\frac{3}{4}$]. Signed and dated in lower l.: *W. Hollar fecit 1660*. Title along the top: *Conventualis Ecclesiae Hospitalis S. Catharinae Juxta Turrim London: a Meridie prospectus*. Dedication of the donor of the plate, *William Petit*, in cartouche upper r. Page number *460* lower r.

Occurs folded in Dugdale, *Monasticon*, Vol. II. (1661), between pp. 460 and 461.

Vertue (IX. 222) also describes a view of *St. Katherine's* of 1672. I have not been able to find it, and perhaps it may be an error of Vertue's.

The Royal Hospital and collegiate church of St. Katherine's, founded by Eleanor, Queen of Henry II, in 1273, and remaining under the patronage of the Queen Consort,[1] existed on the same site until 1825. It was then pulled down to make room for St. Katherine's Dock. The foundation was transferred to Regent's Park, but there are only a few remains of the old church in the new St. Katherine's (*e. g.* part of some of the stalls).

22. THE TOWER.

P. 908.—V. III. 4.—Plate XXXI.

[$5\frac{7}{8} \times 10\frac{1}{8}$, plate line; $5\frac{5}{8} \times 9\frac{7}{8}$, border line].

The title above in the sky: *Castrum Royale Londinense vulgo the Tower*.

I. Before number. Not in British Museum.

II. With marked *8* in margin lower r. (its number in the series which includes my Nos. 26, 28, 79, 85, 86, 90, 107).

From its size and shape, it originally formed a set with Nos. 26, 28 and 79.

A drawing of the Tower, taken from a point rather further away and embracing more buildings at either side, is in the British Museum (see Plate IX).

[1] Though at the moment still in the hands of Queen Alexandra.

23. THE TOWER, WITH THE EXECUTION OF THE EARL OF STRAF-
FORD.

P. 552.—V. II. 34.—Plate XXXI.

[7⅛ × 10⅜]. Signed in lower l.: W H (in monogram).

I. (On same plate as No. 91 below.) Described by Parthey as in the collection of Francis Graves, London. I have not seen an impression.

II. The plate divided, separating the present subject from No. 91.

Title along the top: *The True Maner of the Execution of Thomas Earle of Strafford, Lord Lieutenant of Ireland upon Tower hill, the 12ᵗʰ of May, 1641.*

In upper r. references A to D to the various personages in the scene. Clear margin below.

III. *Execution des Grafen Thomae von Strafford . . . 1641* added in lower margin.

IV. *Hyberniae Proregis Supplicium* added below the upper title.

24. THE TOWER, WITH THE EXECUTION OF THE EARL OF STRAF-
FORD: SMALL PLATE.

Undescribed.

[5 1/16 × 3 15/16. The upper part to border line, 2⅜ × 3¾].

A small plate with two historical subjects. The view described contained in the upper part lettered: *The Earle of Strafford for treasonable practises beheaded on the Tower-hill.*

I. Double plate. Occurs in John Vicars, *A Sight of the Transactions of these latter yeares* [London, 1646], on p. 11.

II. The plate divided in two. The upper part occurs in John Vicars, *True Information of the Beginning and Cause of all our Troubles.* London, 1648, and London, 1648 [1649], on p. 9.

Not signed, but almost certainly by Hollar.

25. THE TOWER, WITH THE IMPRISONED BISHOPS.

Undescribed.

[5 1/16 × 3 15/16. The upper subject to border line, 2⅜ × 3 11/16].

A small plate with two subjects. The subject described contained in the upper part, lettered: *The Bishops imprisoned in the Towre of London for protesting against the Parliament.*

Occurs in John Vicars, *A Sight of the Transactions of these latter years* [London, 1646], on p. 15.

Not signed, but almost certainly by Hollar.

26. ST. MARY OVERY'S, FROM THE SOUTH, WITH ST. PAUL'S IN THE DISTANCE.

P., B. 910.—V. III. 6.—Plate XXX.

[5⅞ × 10 3/16. To border line, 5 11/16 × 9⅞]. Signed and dated in lower r.: *W. Hollar fec: 1647.*

The title in the sky, above : *S. Marie Over's in Southwarke.*

I. Before the number. PRAGUE.

II. The number *1* added in margin lower r. 7 mm. from r. corner of border line (its number in the series composed of Nos. 22, 28, 79, 85, 86, 90, 107).

From its size and shape, it originally formed a set with Nos. 22, 28 and 79.

27. ST. MARY OVERY'S, FROM THE SOUTH.

P. 1033.—V. IX. 183.

[8⅜ × 11¹⁵⁄₁₆]. Signed and dated lower l. : *W: Hollar delin : et sculp:ᵗ 1661.*

Title in cartouche upper l.: *S. Mariae Overie olim Conventualis Ecclesiae ab Austro prospectus.*

The dedication of the donor of the plate Randolph Sheldon in cartouche r.

I. Before number. BRITISH MUSEUM.

II. Page number *940* added in lower r.

Occurs in this state folded in Dugdale, *Monasticon*, Vol. II. (1661), between pp. 940 and 941.

28. THE ROYAL EXCHANGE. INTERIOR: FACING SOUTH.

P. 907.—V. III. 3.—Plate XXXII.

[5⅞ × 10¼. To border line, 5⅝ × 9¹⁵⁄₁₆]. Signed in work below r.: *W. Hollar fecit* (W H in monogram).

The title on scroll in centre above : *Byrsa Londinensis vulgo the Royal Exchange.*

I. Before the number. Not in the British Museum (unless impression cut to the border line be a proof).

II. The number *7* added in lower margin r. (its number in the series which also includes Nos. 22, 26, 79, 85, 86, 90 and 107).

From its size and shape, it originally formed a set with Nos. 22, 26 and 79.

This is the old Exchange, built at the expense of Sir Thomas Gresham between 1566 and 1571. Its general design was suggested by the Burse of Amsterdam. The present print shows the Exchange in holiday, with various groups of citizens, children at play, with whip-tops, etc.

The present Royal Exchange (built 1842–1844) is the second building since Gresham's Exchange. The Exchange as rebuilt after the Fire of London, was itself burnt down in 1838. At the Great Fire the only statue that escaped uninjured was that of the Founder, and his statue again escaped the conflagration of 1838.

29. THE ROYAL EXCHANGE. INTERIOR: FACING WEST.

P., B. 1036.—V. III. 2.—Plate XXXII.

[11⅝ × 15½]. Signed and dated in frame r. below : (in states I. and II.) *W. Hollar fecit Londini, Anno 1644.*

The title in cartouche above: *Byrsa Londinensis vulgo the Royall Exchange of London,* and in two columns ten Latin and ten English verses signed *H. Pecham.*

The English verses are as follows:—

Lo heere the Modell of Magnificence | the Exchange of London thorough Europe fam'd | Erected first by Gresham's greate expence, | And by the Roial'st Queene the Royal nam'd | the mother Antwerp's farre exelling where | But emptiness is seene or trifles sold | Arabian odors, silkes from Seres heere | Pearles, Sables, fine linnen, Iewels, clothes of gold | And what not rare or rich our Kinges take places | Without. Within a World of beauteous faces.

Along the framework at the foot: *This foremost is to be understood for the fourth Walke, being such as the other three, arched and such Pillors as the rest. All which could not bee heere conveniently exprest,* and the signature (as quoted above).

I. Before the medallion with Gresham's head.

The dedication in upper cartouche reads: *Honoratissimo Domino . . . Johanni Wollaston, Equiti . . . Hanc tabulam a Wenceslao Hollar Bohemo delineatam & Aqua forti aeri insculptā ipse Author humillimae* (sic) *dedicat A° 1644.* BRITISH MUSEUM. WINDSOR. PRAGUE. NORTHWICK PARK.

II. Medallion with Gresham's head hung from the cartouche.

In place of *Hanc tabulam . . . A° 1644,* is now read *Itemque Duumviris . . . DDD Ricardus Daynes.* BRITISH MUSEUM.

III. The English arms in place of the dedication in the upper cartouche, and the inscription along the framework at the foot altered to: *This is yͤ Exact Representation of yͤ Royall Exchange as it was before yͤ late fire, 1666, designed and engraven by W. Hollar ; Printed for & sold by Nathanael Brooke, Stationer, at yͤ Angell in Cornehill. A 1668.* WINDSOR.

Shows the Exchange with a large crowd assembled for transaction of business.

30. CORNHILL AND THE OLD EXCHANGE.

P. 609.—Plate VIII.

Forms the background of *Winter* (P. 609), one of the *Four Seasons* illustrated in full-length female costume studies (P. 606–609).

The view is taken from near the E. end of the Poultry looking E. towards the Royal Exchange and Cornhill. The Royal Exchange seems to be shown on the left as well as to the right of the female figure, though too much space is really allowed for the proper length of the façade. The small building in Cornhill in front of the Exchange is the famous "Tun" (so-called from its shape), built in 1283 and used as a prison for night-walkers and other suspicious persons. It formed part of a structure used also as a water conduit.

This background has sometimes been wrongly described as Cheapside.

In all the impressions I have seen the background seems reworked, even when the impressions belong to series in which the other three show no signs of rework. Perhaps Hollar made corrections in his background before issuing the plate.

31. THE CROSS IN CHEAPSIDE.

Undescribed.—Plate XXXIII.

[$4\frac{15}{16} \times 3\frac{3}{4}$. The upper subject to border line, $2\frac{13}{16} \times 3\frac{5}{8}$].

A small plate with two subjects. The subject described contained in the upper part lettered: *The 2 of May 1643. Yᵉ Crosse in Cheapeside was pulled downe, a Troope of Horse and 2 Companies of foote wayted to garde it and at yᵉ fall of yᵉ tope Crosse drõmes beat trũpets blew and multitudes of Capes wayre throwne in yᵉ Ayre and a greate Shoute of People with joy, yᵉ 2. of May the Almanake sayeth, was yᵉ invention of the Crosse, and 6 day at night was the Leaden Popes burnt, in the place where it stood with ringinge of Bells, and a greate Acclamation and no hurt done in all these actions.*

Occurs in John Vicars, *A Sight of the Transactions of these latter yeares* [London 1646] on p. 21, and in John Vicars, *True Information of the Beginning and Cause of all our Troubles*, London 1648, and London 1648 [1649], on p. 17.

Not signed, but almost certainly by Hollar.

Cheapside and the Cross are illustrated in another contemporary etching showing the cortège of Marie de Médicis on her visit to her daughter Henrietta Maria in 1638 (which appeared in Jean Puget de la Serre, *Histoire de l'Entrée de la Regne Mère du Roy Très Chrestien dans la Grande-Bretaigne:* London, 1639, fol.

It was one of the twelve crosses erected by Edward I in memory of his queen Eleanor, at each of the places her body rested between Hardeby (near Lincoln) where she died in 1290, and Westminster Abbey. Waltham, Cheapside, and Charing were the last on the route. The Cross was rebuilt in the fifteenth century at the instigation of John Hatherley, Lord Mayor.

32. OLD ST. PAUL'S. GROUND PLAN OF THE CRYPT (ST. FAITH).

P. 1029.—V. IX. 268.—Plate XXXIV.

[$7\frac{7}{8} \times 11\frac{7}{8}$]. Signed and dated lower r.: *W. Hollar delin: et sculp: 1657.*

Title in centre above: *Templi Parochialis S. Fidis (scil. areae ejusdem) Ichnographia.*

I. In lower l. the page number, *114.* Occurs in Dugdale, *St. Paul's*, 1658, on p. 114.

II. Worn and reworked. Page number altered to *116.* In Dugdale, *St. Paul's*, 1716, on p. 116.

This and the following, Nos. 33–67, were all (except No. 43) illustrations in Dugdale, *St. Paul's*, 1658, and a few (Nos. 35, 36, 37, 39, 41) were used later in Dugdale's *Monasticon*, Vol. III. (1673).

33. OLD ST. PAUL'S. VIEW OF THE CRYPT (ST. FAITH).

P. 1030.—V. IX. 269.—Plate XXXV.

[$7\frac{7}{8} \times 13\frac{5}{8}$]. Signed in lower r.: *W. Hollar delin: et sculp:*

Title in compartment along upper border : *Ecclesiae Parochialis S^{tae} Fidis Prospectus interior.*

I. In lower l. the page number, *115*, and in lower r., *116*. Occurs in Dugdale, *St. Paul's*, 1658, as p. 115 (or pp. 115 and 116). The plate is rather too large for the page, unless a large margin is given, and it is slightly cut in the Grenville copy. The two numbers probably indicate the original idea of placing it as a folding plate.

II. The number in lower r. altered to *117*. In Dugdale, *St. Paul's*, 1716, as p. 117 (or pp. 117 and 118).

34. OLD ST. PAUL'S. THE CHAPTER HOUSE.

P. 1023.—V. IX. 271.—Plate XXXVIII.

[7¾ × 11¼]. Signed in lower r. : *W. Hollar delineavit et sculpsit.*
The title in compartment above : *Domus Capitularis S.^{ti} Pauli, a Meridie Prospectus.*
I. In upper l. the page number, *127*. Occurs in Dugdale, *St. Paul's*, 1658, folded between pp. 126 and 127.
II. Rework, and added work ; the number altered to *P. 128*. In Dugdale, *St. Paul's*, 1716, between pp. 128 and 129.

35. SOUTH VIEW OF OLD ST. PAUL'S, WITH THE SPIRE.

P. 1017.—V. IX. 272.—Plate XXXV.

[10 × 13½]. Signed and dated below towards r. : *W. Hollar sculp: 1657.*
Title in compartment upper l. : *Ecclesiae Paulinae Prospectus qualis olim erat prinsquam eius pyramis e coelo tacta conflagraverat.*
I. In upper l. the page number, *133*. Occurs in Dugdale, *St. Paul's*, 1658, folded, between pp. 132 and 133.
II. In lower l. the page number, *297*. Occurs in Dugdale, *Monasticon*, Vol. III. (1673), folded, between pp. 296 and 297.

The plate in Dugdale, *St. Paul's*, 1716, is a copy engraved by John Harris.

The spire of Old St. Paul's was struck by lightning and burnt in 1561. What remained was then pulled down, and the square tower remained temporarily roofed in until the Great Fire. The roof of the nave was also considerably damaged at the same time.

36. GROUND PLAN OF OLD ST. PAUL'S.

P. 1016.—V. IX. 273.—Plate XXXIV.

[9¼ × 13¾]. Signed and dated in lower l. : *Wenceslaus Hollar dimensit, delineavit et aqua forti aeri insculpsit A^o 1657.*
Title above : *Area Ecclesiae Cathedralis S.^{ti} Pauli Ichnographia.*
I. In upper l. the page number, *161*. In Dugdale, *St. Paul's*, 1658, folded, as p. 161.

II. In lower l. the page number, *297.* In Dugdale, *Monasticon*, Vol. III. (1673), folded between pp. 296 and 297.

The plate in Dugdale, *St. Paul's,* 1716, is a copy engraved by John Harris.

37. OLD ST. PAUL'S. THE EXTERIOR: SOUTH.

P. 1018.—V. IX. 274.—Plate XXXVI.

[8 × 14⅞]. Signed below, towards r.: *W. Hollar delin: et sculp:*
Title in cartouche upper l.: *Ecclesiae Cathedralis S.ti Pauli a Meridie Prospectus.*
I. In upper l. the page number, *162.* In Dugdale, *St. Paul's,* 1658, folded, as p. 162.
II. In lower l. the page number, *297.* In Dugdale, *Monasticon*, Vol. III. (1673), folded, between pp. 296 and 297.

38. OLD ST. PAUL'S. EXTERIOR: NORTH.

P. 1019.—V. IX. 275.—Plate XXXVI.

[7⅞ × 14⅞]. Signed and dated in lower l.: *W. Hollar delineavit et sculp: Londini, 1656.*
Title in cartouche above r.: *Ecclesiae Cathedralis S. Pauli A Septentrione Prospectus.*
I. In upper l. the page number, *163.* In Dugdale, *St. Paul's,* 1658, folded, as p. 163.
II. Reworked. In Dugdale, *St. Paul's,* 1716 (according to "Directions to the Binder," between pp. 134 and 135).

Daniel King etched the same subject after Hollar's drawing for Dodsworth and Dugdale's *Monasticon*, Vol. I. (1655), which appeared also in his own series of the *Cathedrall and Conventuall Churches of England and Wales,* 1656.

39. OLD ST. PAUL'S. EXTERIOR: WEST.

P. 1020.—V. IX. 276.—Plate XXXVII.

[9 × 10⅝]. Signed towards r. below: *W. Hollar delin: et sculp:*
Title in cartouche upper l.: *Ecclesiae Cathedralis S.ti Pauli ab Occidente Prospectus.*
I. In upper l. the page number, *164.* In Dugdale, *St. Paul's,* 1658, folded, as p. 164.
II. In lower l. the page number, *297.* In Dugdale, *Monasticon*, Vol. III. (1673), folded, between pp. 296 and 297.

The plate in Dugdale, *St. Paul's,* 1716, is a copy engraved by John Harris.
Shows the classic portico designed by Inigo Jones in 1633.

40. OLD ST. PAUL'S. EXTERIOR: EAST END.

P. 1021.—V. IX. 277.

[9¾ × 6¾]. Signed and dated in centre below: *W. Hollar delineavit et sculpsit 1656.*
Title above: *Ecclesiae Cathedralis Sti Pauli Orientalis Facies.*

I. Before signature, and other lettering. BRITISH MUSEUM.

II. In upper l. the page number, *165*. In Dugdale, *St. Paul's*, 1658, as p. 165.

This is not reproduced as it merely gives part of No. 41 on a somewhat larger scale.

41. OLD ST. PAUL'S. EXTERIOR: EAST.

P. 1022.—V. IX. 278.—Plate XXXVII.

[7⅝ × 9⅝]. Signed below r.: *W. Hollar delin: et sculp:*

Title above: *Ecclesiae Cathedralis S^{ti} Pauli Lond: ab Oriente Prospectus.*

I. Cartouche upper r. blank. Also an empty cartouche upper l. WINDSOR.

II. Dedication of the donor *John Walpoole* added in cartouche upper r., and coat of arms added in place of the empty cartouche l. In upper l. the page number, *166*. In Dugdale, *St. Paul's*, 1658, folded, as p. 166.

III. In lower l. the page number, *297*. In Dugdale, *Monasticon*, Vol. III. (1673), folded, between pp. 296 and 297.

The plate in Dugdale, *St. Paul's*, 1716, is a copy engraved by John Harris.

42. OLD ST. PAUL'S. INTERIOR: THE NAVE.

P. 1025.—V. IX. 279.—Plate XXXIX.

[15¾ × 13⅞]. Signed at foot of margin below: *Wenceslaus Hollar Bohemus hujus Ecclesiae quotidie casum expectantis delineator et olim admirator memoriam sic preservavit A° 1658.*

The title above: *Navis Ecclesiae Cathedralis S. Pauli Prospectus Interior.*

In the margin the inscription: *Sit rediviva mater Ecclesia et pereant Sacrilegi ut navis Ecclesiae temporum fluctibus immersura salutaribus Dei auspiciis conservetur. Majorum pietatem imitando mirentur posteri ut stupenda haec Basilica antiquitus fundata et jamjam collapsura, tamquam sacrum Religionis Christianae Monumentum in aeternum sufflaminetur.*

I. In upper l. the page number, *167*. Occurs in Dugdale, *St. Paul's*, 1658, folded, as p. 167.

II. The number altered to *145*. In Dugdale, *St. Paul's*, 1716 (according to "Directions to the Binder," between pp. 134 and 135).

Both Hollar's signature, and the marginal lettering are curiously interesting in relation to the state of the fabric of St. Paul's, and the restoration thought of in the period just preceding the Great Fire. Since the Fire of 1561 the roof of the nave, as well as that of the tower, had only been temporarily repaired with boards and lead, and money was collected at various times between then and 1666 for restoration. During the Civil Wars and Commonwealth the Cathedral had been used by the soldiers for stabling, and the fabric had no doubt been entirely disregarded.

Compare the inscription to No. 46 below.

43. OLD ST. PAUL'S. INTERIOR: THE NAVE. SMALLER PLATE.

Undescribed.

[$11\frac{15}{16} \times 8\frac{5}{8}$].

Title above: *Navis Ecclesiae Cathedralis S. Pauli Lond: Prospectus interior.*
Dedication of donor of the plate, Philip Howard, son of Henry Howard, Earl of Arundel, in oval cartouche upper r. BRITISH MUSEUM.

This plate, which is unsigned, shows faults of biting on the floor of the nave. It may have been on that account that Hollar rejected it, and made another plate for Dugdale. As the donor's name is already affixed, it was no doubt intended originally for the book.

44. OLD ST. PAUL'S. INTERIOR: THE EXTERIOR OF THE CHOIR, FROM THE WEST.

P. 1024.—V. IX. 280.—Plate XXXVIII.

[$9\frac{3}{16} \times 12\frac{3}{4}$]. Signed below l.: *W. Hollar delineavit et sculp:*
Title above: *Partis exterioris Chori ab Occidente prospectus.*
Verses from the *Iliad*, and from the *Aeneid* in the margin.
I. Before the page number.
II. In upper r. the page number, *168.* Occurs in Dugdale, *St. Paul's*, 1658, folded, as p. 168. (The Grenville copy of this edition contains State I. with number in MS.)
III. The number changed to *146.* In Dugdale, *St. Paul's*, 1716 (according to "Directions to the Binder," between pp. 134 and 135).

45. OLD ST. PAUL'S. INTERIOR: THE CHOIR, FACING EAST.

P. 1026.—V. IX. 281.—Plate XL.

[$12\frac{1}{2} \times 8\frac{7}{8}$]. Signed below l.: *Wenceslaus Hollar delineavit et sculpsit.*
Title above: *Chori Ecclesiae Cathedralis S. Pauli Prospectus Interior.*
I. In upper l. the page number, *169.* In Dugdale, *St. Paul's*, 1658, folded, as p. 169.
II. Page number altered to *147.* Occurs in Dugdale, *St. Paul's*, 1716 (according to "Directions to the Binder," between pp. 134 and 135).

46. OLD ST. PAUL'S. INTERIOR: EAST END.

P. 1027.—V. IX. 282.—Plate XLI.

[$12 \times 8\frac{3}{8}$]. Signed below toward the l.: *W. Hollar fecit.*
Title in margin below: *Orientalis Partis Eccl: Cath: S: Pauli, Prospectus Interior.*
In compartment in centre below, the Latin inscription: *Ecclesiae Paulinae moles sacra Pietatis avitae documentum, Senio, et sacrilego ruitura, sequioris seculi opprobrium— Tantum Relligio potuit—*
I. In upper l. the page number, *170.* In Dugdale, *St. Paul's*, 1658, folded, as p. 170.

II. The page number altered to *148*. Occurs in Dugdale, *St. Paul's*, 1716 (according to "Directions to the Binder," between pp. 134 and 135).

The Latin inscription again emphasis the condition of the building (cf. No. 42 above).

47. OLD ST. PAUL'S. CHAPEL OF THOMAS KEMPE, BISHOP OF LONDON.

P. 2309.—V. IX. 270.

[$9\frac{3}{16} \times 10\frac{1}{8}$].

Title above, in centre: *Capella Thomae Kempe Lond. Ep. in qua tumulus suus quondan exstitit. Inter Navim Ecclesiae et alam borealem.*

In upper l. the page number, *40*. In Dugdale, *St. Paul's*, 1658, folded, between pp. 40 and 41, and in edition 1716 between pp. 42 and 43 (according to "Directions to the Binder").

Thomas Kempe was Bishop of London, 1450–1480.
Not signed, but certainly by Hollar.
None of the monuments in Old St. Paul's, illustrated in this and the following numbers, survived the Great Fire, except the tomb of Dr. Donne (see No. 50 below).

48. OLD ST. PAUL'S. THE TOMB OF SIR JOHN DE BEAUCHAMP.

P. 2248.—V. IX. 283.

[$10\frac{3}{8} \times 7\frac{1}{4}$]. Signed below in centre: *W. Hollar fecit.*

Above in centre the title: *Inter Ecclesiae navim et alam Australem Tumulus Iohannis de Bellocampo militis, Ordinis Garterij praenobilis unius fundatorum.*

In upper l. the page number, *52*. In Dugdale, *St. Paul's*, 1658 and 1716, on p. 52.

Sir John de Beauchamp, K.G. (*d.* 1360), was son of Guy, Earl of Warwick.

49. OLD ST. PAUL'S. TOMBS (SLABS) OF BISHOP ROBERT FITZHUGH, WILLIAM GRENE, AND DEAN EVERE.

P. 2290.—V. IX. 299.

[$10\frac{3}{4} \times 7\frac{1}{16}$].

Above to l. the tomb of FitzHugh, described as *In superiori parte Chori prope Altare;* to r. the tomb of William Grene, described as *In medio Chori prope Altare;* below, the tomb of Dean Evere, described as *In Choro prope introitum.*

In upper l. the page number, *60*. In Dugdale, *St. Paul's*, 1658 and 1716, on p. 60.

Not signed, but certainly by Hollar.
Robert FitzHugh, Bishop of London, 1431–1436.

50. OLD ST. PAUL'S. SEPULCHRAL MONUMENT OF JOHN DONNE, WITH EFFIGY OF DONNE IN HIS SHROUD.

P. 2277.—V. IX. 284.

$[11\frac{7}{8} \times 6\frac{3}{8}]$.

The monument is described above as *Inter Chorum et alam australem.*

In upper l. the page number, *62.* In Dugdale, *St. Paul's*, 1658 and 1716, on p. 62.

Not signed, but certainly by Hollar.
The only monumental effigy in St. Paul's left whole by the Great Fire.
Dr. John Donne, Poet, Divine, and Dean of St. Paul's (1573–1631).

51. OLD ST. PAUL'S. TOMBS (SLABS) OF BISHOP JOHN KING, JOHN ACTON, AND SIMON EDOLPH.

P. 2236.—V. IX. 285.

$[11 \times 7\frac{1}{2}]$. Signed in centre below: *W. Hollar fec.*

In upper l. the page number, *72.* In Dugdale, *St. Paul's*, 1658 and 1716, on p. 72.

52. OLD ST. PAUL'S. TOMBS OF THOMAS OKEFORD, WILLIAM RYTHYN, AND RICHARD LITCHFIELD (LICHFIELD).

P. 2322.—V. IX. 286.

$[11\frac{7}{8} \times 6\frac{3}{8}]$. Signed in centre below: *W. Hollar fecit.*

In upper l. the page number, *74.* In Dugdale, *St. Paul's*, 1658 and 1716, on p. 74.

53. OLD ST. PAUL'S. TOMBS (SLABS) OF WILLIAM WORSLEY (DEAN), ROGER BRABAZON, AND VALENTINE CAREY (DEAN).

P. 2377.—V. IX. 287.

$[9\frac{1}{4} \times 7\frac{7}{8}]$.

In upper l. corner the page number, *76.* In Dugdale, *St. Paul's*, 1658 and 1716, on p. 76.

Not signed, but certainly by Hollar.
Valentine Carey, Dean of St. Paul's, later Bishop of Exeter. His Life by Isaac Walton.

54. OLD ST. PAUL'S. TOMBS (SLABS) OF JOHN NEWCOURT, AND OF ANOTHER UNNAMED.

P. 2320.—V. IX. 288.

$[10\frac{1}{4} \times 7\frac{1}{4}]$. Signed in centre below: *W. Hollar fecit.*

In upper l. corner the page number, *78.* In Dugdale, *St. Paul's*, 1658 and 1716, on p. 78.

55. OLD ST. PAUL'S. TOMBS OF HENRY DE WINGHAM (WENGHAM), AND EUSTACE DE FAUCONBERGE.

P. 2361.—V. IX. 289.

[$8\frac{5}{16} \times 10\frac{13}{16}$]. Signed: *W. Hollar delin: et sculp:*
In upper l. the page number, *80* (the same also lightly scratched in upper r.). In Dugdale, *St. Paul's*, 1658 and 1716, on p. 80.

> Recumbent figures under a single Gothic canopy.
> Henry de Wingham, Bishop of London (*d.* 1262)
> Eustace de Fauconberge, Bishop of London (1221–1229).

56. OLD ST. PAUL'S. TOMBS OF HENRY DE LACY (LACIE) AND ROBERT DE BRAYBROKE.

P. 2311.—V. IX. 290.

[$10\frac{7}{8} \times 7\frac{1}{4}$]. Signed: *W. Hollar delin: et sculp.*
In Dugdale, *St. Paul's*, 1658 and 1716, on p. 84.

> The monument of Henry de Lacy shows a recumbent figure on tomb, that of Braybroke a slab.
> Henry de Lacy, Earl of Lincoln, was Protector in the absence of Edward I.
> Robert de Braybroke, Bishop of London (1382–1405).

57. OLD ST. PAUL'S. TOMB OF ROGER NIGER.

P. 2336.—V. IX. 291.

[$9\frac{1}{8} \times 6\frac{3}{4}$. With separate plate above with dedication of the donor of the plate, $3\frac{1}{16} \times 6\frac{3}{4}$]. Signed in the centre below: *W. Hollar fecit.*
Above l. (both on principal plate and dedication plate) the page number, *86* (that on principal plate scratched in 1st edition; engraved in 2nd edition). In Dugdale, *St. Paul's*, 1658, on p. 86, and the principal plate, ed. 1716, p. 86.
The dedication plate does not appear in the edition of 1716.

> Shows the tomb beneath a Gothic canopy.
> Roger Niger (or Le Noir), Bishop of London (*d.* 1241).

58. OLD ST. PAUL'S. TOMB OF JOHN OF GAUNT AND HIS WIFE.

P. 2292.—V. IX. 292.

[$12\frac{1}{8} \times 6\frac{5}{8}$].
In upper l. the page number, *90*. In Dugdale, *St. Paul's*, 1658 and 1716, on p. 90.

> Not signed, but certainly by Hollar.
> Shows tomb with two recumbent figures beneath a canopy.

59. OLD ST. PAUL'S. TOMBS OF KING SEBBA AND ETHELRED.

P. 2341.—V. IX. 293.

[7⅝ × 10⅛]. Signed in centre below: *W. Hollar delineavit et sculp.*
I. In upper l. the page number, *92*. In Dugdale, *St. Paul's*, 1658, on p. 92.
II. Coarsely reworked. The page number altered to *94*. In Dugdale, *St. Paul's*, 1716, on p. 94.

Shows tombs under low and contiguous arches.

60. OLD ST. PAUL'S. SEPULCHRAL MONUMENT AND EFFIGY OF WILLIAM AUBREY.

P. 2242.—V. IX. 294.

[11⅞ × 6⅝]. Signed in centre below: *W. Hollar delin. et sculp.*
I. In upper l. the page number, *96*. In Dugdale, *St. Paul's*, 1658, on p. 96.
II. Worn, and reworked. In Dugdale, *St. Paul's*, 1716, on p. 96.

William Aubrey, Regius Professor of Law at Oxford: a famous lawyer (*d.* 1595).

61. OLD ST. PAUL'S. TOMB OF JOHN DE CHISHULL.

P. 2264.—V. IX. 295.

[6¾ × 9¼]. Signed in lower r.: *W. Hollar delin. et sculp.*
In lower l. the page number, *98*. In Dugdale, *St. Paul's*, 1658, on p. 98, and edition 1716, on p. 100.

The tomb is under an arched recess.
John de Chishull, Bishop of London (*d.* 1280).

62. OLD ST. PAUL'S. TOMB OF RALPH DE HENGHAM.

P. 2301.—V. IX. 296.

[11 × 7⅜]. Signed in centre below: *W. Hollar delin. et sculp.*
I. In upper l. the page number, *100*. In Dugdale, *St. Paul's*, 1658, on p. 100.
II. The number altered to *102*. In Dugdale, *St. Paul's*, 1716, on p. 102.

Showing tomb in arched recess and also the face of slab.
Ralph de Hengham, judge and ecclesiastic (*d.* 1311).

63. OLD ST. PAUL'S. TOMB OF SIR SIMON BURLEY.

P. 2255.—V. IX. 297.

[11 × 7⅜]. Signed in centre below: *W. Hollar delineavit et sculpsit.*
I. In upper l. the page number, *102*. In Dugdale, *St. Paul's*, 1658, on p. 102.

II. Worn and reworked. Page number altered to *104*. In Dugdale, *St. Paul's*, 1716, on p. 104.

> Shows recumbent figure on tomb beneath a canopy.
> Sir Simon Burley (1336–1388).

64. OLD ST. PAUL'S. TOMB (SLAB) OF JOHN MULLINS AND MARBLE TABLET TO SIR SIMON BASKERVILLE.

P. 2319.

[10¾ × 6⅛].
I. In upper l. the page number, *104*. In Dugdale, *St. Paul's*, 1658, on p. 104.
II. The number altered to *106*. In Dugdale, *St. Paul's*, 1716, on p. 106.

> Not signed, but certainly by Hollar.
> John Mullins (Molyns), Archdeacon of London (*d.* 1591).
> Sir Simon Baskerville, Physician to James I and Charles I (*d.* 1641).

65. OLD ST. PAUL'S. TOMB OF SIR JOHN WOLLEY.

P. 2375.

[10½ × 7¼].
I. In upper l. the page number, *106*. In Dugdale, *St. Paul's*, 1658, on p. 106.
II. The number altered to *108*. In Dugdale, *St. Paul's*, 1716, on p. 108.

> Not signed, but certainly by Hollar.
> On the tomb are seated effigies of Wolley, his wife and son.
> Sir John Wolley, Latin Secretary to Queen Elizabeth (*d.* 1596).

66. OLD ST. PAUL'S. SEPULCHRAL MONUMENT AND EFFIGY OF ALEXANDER NOWELL.

P. 2321.

[10⅝ × 6⅝].
I. Before the page number. In Dugdale, *St. Paul's*, 1658, on p. 110.
II. Page number *112* added, upper l. In Dugdale, *St. Paul's*, 1716, on p. 112.

> Not signed, but certainly by Hollar.
> Alexander Nowell, Dean of St. Paul's (*b.* 1507?, *d.* 1602).

67. OLD ST. PAUL'S. SHRINE OF ST. ERKENWALD.

P. 2286.—V. IX. 298.

[9½ × 6⅞]. Signed in lower r.: *W. Hollar fecit 1657*.
I. In upper l. the page number, *112*. In Dugdale, *St. Paul's*, 1658, on p. 112.
II. The page number altered to *114*. In Dugdale, *St. Paul's*, 1716, on p. 114.

> St. Erkenwald, Bishop of London (*d.* 693).

68. OLD ST. PAUL'S ON FIRE.

P. 1028 and 2687.

[$2\frac{5}{16} \times 4\frac{1}{8}$]. Signed and dated in lower l.: *W. Hollar fecit A° 1666.*
In centre above: *Etiam periere Ruinae.*

I. On title page of William Sancroft, *Lex Ignea, or the School of Righteousness. A sermon preach'd before the King Octob. 10 1666. At the solemn Feast appointed for the late Fire in London* (Printed for Timothy Garthwait) 1666.

II. A scroll added round the inscription *Etiam periere Ruinae.* Worn and reworked: the signature almost invisible. On title page of same book, in edition printed for R. Pawlett, London, n.d. (Plomer dates Pawlett 1660–1667, so that this edition probably followed very soon after the first. A very large number of copies of the first edition must have been issued for the plate to have become so worn).

Archbishop Sancroft was Dean of St. Paul's at the time of the Great Fire.

69. OLD ST. PAUL'S WITH THE SPIRE, AND PART OF LONDON FROM THE NORTH.

Forms background of P. 530, V. II. 46 (Tournaments of John de Astley). The second tournament with Sir Philip Boyle was at Smithfield 1441, and shows the present view.

I. The page number, *73*, in upper left. Occurs folded in Dugdale, *Antiquities of Warwickshire*, London, 1656, between pp. 72 and 73.

II. *Pag. 110 and 111* added upper l. Worn and reworked. In Dugdale, *Warwickshire*, 2nd edition, 1730 fol., Vol. I., between pp. 110 and 111.

III. More worn, and further reworked. In Dugdale, *Warwickshire*, 3rd edition, Coventry, 1765, Vol. I. (Mounted between pp. 74 and 75 in British Museum Library copy).

70. THE PRIORY OF ST. JOHN OF JERUSALEM.

P. 1031.—V. IX. 221.—Plate XLII.

[$12\frac{3}{4} \times 14\frac{3}{4}$]. Signed and dated [lower l. of piece (*a*)]: *Wenceslaus Hollar delin: et sculp: 1661.*

Showing three views of the Hospital. The plate is divided into three strips: above are the arms and dedication of the donor of the plate, Thomas Baron Bruce; in the centre two views of the hospital (*a*) [on left] with title, *Hospitalariorum Militum Sti Joh: Hierosol: Domus olim excelsae in suburbio civitatis Londin: portae Australis a Circio prospectus,* (*b*) [on right] with title, *Ejusdem Domus (quanti nunc superest) cum occidentali Capellae facie, ab Affrico prospectus;* and in the lower strip a third view of the hospital with title, *Praefatae Domus, à retrò ab Euro-aquilone, prospectus.* In upper r. the page number, *504*. In Dodsworth and Dugdale, *Monasticon*, Vol. II. (1661), between pp. 504 and 505 (folded).

F

The Priory, or Hospital, of St. John of Jerusalem was founded in 1100 by Jordan Briset and his wife; and endowed in 1324 with the revenues of the English Knights Templars. The Order was suppressed by Henry VIII in 1541, and the buildings were afterwards in private hands.

The crypt of St. John's, Clerkenwell, and St. John's Gate (the South Gateway to the Priory as shown in piece *a* of the etching) are the only relics of the old buildings.

71. THE HOLLOW ELM OF HAMPSTEAD.

P. 979.—V. III. 70.

[$7\frac{1}{8} \times 7\frac{3}{4}$. To border line, $6\frac{3}{8} \times 7\frac{9}{16}$]. Signed and dated in lower l. : *W. Hollar delin: et sculp: 1653.*

I. Before flock of birds about the tree : the turret only contains five people (including one whose head alone is seen): the margin blank. BRITISH MUSEUM. (Impression with contemporary MS. inscription in the margin : *Ye* (?) *Tree 26 ft Diam:*[tr] *Langley Park near Windsor.*)

II. Flock of birds added about the tree : the turret now contains six people.

Descriptive lettering added in the margin with eight reference numbers to the print, in three columns : *1. The Bottom above Ground in Compass is—28 foote. 2—3—4—| 8—11—18—19. The Seat above the Stepps | Six may Sitt on, and round about roome for fourteene more All the way you goe up within the Hollow Tree.* BRITISH MUSEUM. WINDSOR.

One of the impressions at Windsor is on a broadside (as described in the Towneley Sale catalogue, possibly from the impression now at Windsor), *printed by E. Cotes, for M. S. at the Blue Bible, in Green Arbour, and are to be given or sold on the Hollow Tree at Hampsted*, and containing among other matter English verses by Robert Codrington, signed and dated July 24, 1653. Vertue, probably following the old MS. inscription on the impression now in the British Museum, described the tree as in Langley Park, near Windsor. Parthey also entitles it " The Hollow Tree at Hampsted near Windsor." But there seems little doubt from the verses by Robert Codrington that the elm must have been on Hampstead Heath, and the idea of height given to the foreground of the etching hardly favours the other locality.

Mr. Thomas J. Barratt refers to the print in his *Annals of Hampstead* (London, 1912, Vol. I. p. 168), but makes no reference to the earlier identification being that of Langley Park, near Windsor.

72. BY THE WATERHOUSE.

P. 915.—V. III. 15.—Plate XLIV.

[$3\frac{5}{8} \times 4\frac{7}{8}$. To border line, $3\frac{1}{4} \times 4\frac{11}{16}$]. Signed and dated in lower margin r.: *W. Hollar delin: et sculp: 1665.*

The title, *by the Waterhouse*, in centre of margin below.

I. Before added work.

II. Heavy cross-hatchings added with the graver r. of bank in the foreground.

The Waterhouse is the New River Head. The New River, constructed with the object of bringing a supply of water to London from springs near Ware (Herts.), was completed and the Waterhouse built in 1613. Hugh Myddelton, to whose enterprise the undertaking was due, and successfully carried out, was made a baronet in 1622.

In the present view the spectator is looking S.E.

Nos. 72–77 form a series of Islington (or more strictly Clerkenwell) views.

Parthey says that later impressions of the whole series bear Overton's address. But I have only seen his address on No. 77. They are rare in good early state, but often met in badly re-worked impressions. I have described states only where I have noted actual differences in line or inscription.

73. BY ISLINGTON (WITH OLD ST. PAUL'S IN THE DISTANCE).

P. 916.—V. III. 16.—Plate XLV.

[3⅝ × 5. To border line, 3¼ × 4⅞]. Signed and dated in lower margin r.: *W: Hollar delin: et sculp: 1665.*

The title, *By Islington*, in centre of margin below.

The church tower furthest r. is St. Sepulchre's. The tower with the turret just to the l. of St. Paul's, probably St. Bartholomew the Less.

Further l., showing over the large shed, St. Mary-le-Bow, and the higher of the two towers l. might be St. Michael's, Cornhill, though the pinnacles of the tower are by no means faithfully drawn.

The view is taken within about a hundred yards to the W. of the Waterhouse. The ditch which turns a corner in the foreground (a corner seen in the following print) seems to be a small overflow from the New River Head, which may have joined the Fleet Ditch. But I do not find it marked on any map of the period.

The barn-like building in the middle distance is what was called the *London Spa* (or *Spaw*, as it was sometimes spelt), one of the few mineral springs in the north of London, used also as a sort of restaurant in the seventeenth or eighteenth century.[1]

It appears in the same condition on a *New and Exact Prospect of the North Side of the City of London taken from the Upper Pond near Islington Aug 5 1730*, engraved by T. B[owles] (Crace collection, British Museum). The toll house on the right is in about the position of the "Ducking Pond House" in Bowles's view, but if it is this house it was considerably altered and enlarged by 1730. It is, on the other hand, not unlike a narrow house entitled *White's Conduit* in an engraving (by C. Lemprière?) of 1731.

[1] See Philip Norman *London Signs and Inscriptions* : London, 1893, p. 190.

74. BY ISLINGTON (WITH THE WATERHOUSE).

P. 917.—V. III. 17.—Plate XLIII.

[$3\frac{9}{16} \times 4\frac{15}{16}$. To border line, $3\frac{1}{4} \times 4\frac{13}{16}$]. Signed and dated in lower margin l.: *W. Hollar delin: et sculp: 1665.*
The title, *By Islington*, in centre of margin below.

The spectator is here looking E.
The ditch in the foreground seems to be the same overflow from the New River Head shown in the preceding view.

75. ON THE NORTH SIDE OF LONDON (WITH OLD ST. PAUL'S IN THE DISTANCE).

P. 918.—V. III. 18.—Plate XLV.

[$3\frac{1}{2} \times 5$. To border line, $3\frac{1}{4} \times 4\frac{13}{16}$]. Signed and dated in lower margin r.: *W Hollar* (W H in monogram) *delin: et sculp: 1665.*
The title, *On the North side of London*, in centre of lower margin.

A similar view to No. 73, but taken from a point a few hundred yards further west. St. Sepulchre's shows on a line with the W. front of St. Paul's. The lower tower further W. probably St. Andrew's, Holborn. Left of St. Paul's, St. Bartholomew the Less, and St. Mary-le-Bow, and the high tower near the l. margin probably St. Michael's, Cornhill.

76. THE WATERHOUSE BY ISLINGTON.

P. 919.—V. III. 19.—Plate XLIII.

[$3\frac{9}{16} \times 4\frac{15}{16}$. To border line, $3\frac{1}{4} \times 4\frac{3}{4}$]. Signed and dated in lower margin r.: *W. Hollar delin: et sculp: 1665.*
The title, *Waterhouse by Islington*, in centre of lower margin.

I. Before added work.
II. Heavy cross-hatchings added with the graver in the ditch in the foreground.

The spectator is here looking E. The beginning of the overflow from the New River Head is here clearly shown.

77. YE WATERHOUSE.

P., B. 920.—V. III. 20.—Plate XLIV.

[$3\frac{9}{16} \times 5$. To border line, $3\frac{1}{4} \times 4\frac{13}{16}$]. Signed and dated in margin lower r.: *W. Hollar* (W H in monogram) *fecit 1665.*
The title, *Yᵉ Waterhouse*, in centre of lower margin.
I. Before Overton's address. NORTHWICK PARK.
II. *Sould by John Ouerton* added in lower margin l.

The spectator is here looking S. In the middle distance, about 200 yards S. of the Waterhouse is the "London Spa." The towers in the distance going from right to left are : St. Andrew's, Holborn, St. Sepulchre's, and St. Paul's (between the "London Spa" and the Waterhouse), and St. Mary-le-Bow to the left of the Waterhouse.

78. LINCOLN'S INN FIELDS.

Plate XLVI.

[$3\frac{1}{2} \times 15\frac{9}{10}$, from cut impression].
Double border line.
Title above, *Prospect of Lincoln's Inn Fields from E.N.E.*.

Only known impression (from the coll. of the late Mr. H. Fancourt, of High Barnet) was acquired in 1914 by the BRITISH MUSEUM. It only shows border lines at foot and r., and has probably been slightly cut above and on l. Border line made up on l.

Described and reproduced in *L.C.C. Survey of London*, Vol. III. "Parish of St. Giles-in-the-Fields," by W. Edward Riley and Sir Laurence Gomme: London, 1912 (p. 15, and pl. 6).

It was also described by Mr. H. Fancourt in *The Athenæum*, October 26, 1895, and reproduced in C. W. Heckethorn, *Lincoln's Inn Fields :* London, 1896.

The etching is not signed, but I have no doubt of Hollar's authorship.

A band of mounted soldiers with a standard is shown approaching from the left, preceded by two trumpeters and an officer. Various small groups of civilians about the Fields, and in the background trained bands being drilled. The costume points to a date of about 1640–1660, and the presence of soldiers and trained bands suggests the period of the Civil Wars. The etching shows the Fields before they were laid out with railed walks, as seen in a picture belonging to the Earl of Pembroke (of about 1683). This would indicate a date before 1660, as the Fields were so laid out within a few years after 1657.

The view of the houses surrounding the Fields has caused topographers very considerable difficulty, and inclined them to regard the print in part as the reproduction of some projected design for building rather than a direct representation of the Square as it existed at any particular date.

In Hollar's *Bird's-eye Plan of the West Central District of London* (No. 6 above), and in the Earl of Pembroke's picture, the houses on the N. side of the Fields are shown without pilasters. On the other hand, a regular succession of pilasters is shown in the present etching on the N. side (r. hand of print), a detail that never existed on the houses on this side of the Square. It is argued in the *L.C.C. Survey of London* that after etching a correct representation of such part of the houses as was erected by about 1658 in the *West Central District Plan*, Hollar would hardly have introduced this variation from actual facts. In another detail, *i.e.* in the form of the archway on the W.

side of the Fields (which was built by about 1641), Hollar appears to be unfaithful, for one can hardly in this case suppose the etching to be done before erection from projected designs. Admitting, then, that Hollar was not so far in advance of contemporary topographers to be faithful to architectural detail, I do not think that it is entirely improbable that he would have introduced even so consistent a deflection from the truth as this series of pilasters to make the newer northern side uniform in style with the façades on the west, and it is easy to imagine him omitting to show the break in the elevation of the roofs of the buildings on the N. side (a break which is clearly shown in the Earl of Pembroke's picture). If then Hollar's inaccuracy is admitted, one might date the etching about 1658–1660. On the other hand, two suggestions have been made. Heckethorne (*Lincoln's Inn Fields*, p. 102) regarded the Hollar print as a reproduction of a design by Inigo Jones for the Square, but there is no actual record that Inigo Jones ever made a regular design for the whole Square. The editors of the *Survey of London* think that the etching is more likely to reproduce some sketch of intended building operations (done perhaps as an advertisement by the builder) either (i) about 1641, when William Newton was meditating completion of the Square (the W. and S.W. portion being nearly finished), or (ii) about 1653, when Arthur Newman had purchased the land on the N. side for building.

79. THE PIAZZA IN COVENT GARDEN.

P. 909.—V. III. 5.—Plate XLVII.

[$5\frac{7}{8} \times 10\frac{1}{8}$. To border line, $5\frac{5}{8} \times 9\frac{15}{16}$]. Signed in work in lower r.: *W. Hollar* (W H in monogram) *fecit.*
Title, *Piazza in Covent Garden*, above.
I. Before the number. Not in British Museum.
II. The number *2* added in margin lower r.
Belongs in this state to the series which includes Nos. 22, 26, 28, 79, 85, 86, 90, 107.

From its size and shape it originally formed a set with Nos. 22, 26 and 28.

This shows the Piazza in an earlier state than in the *Bird's-eye Plan of the West Central District* (No. 6 above), where the Square is completely fenced in (in place of the posts in the present etching) and a tree appears in the centre. It is probably among Hollar's early London views (*i. e.* about 1640). In or about 1668 a column with a dial at its head was erected in the centre of the Piazza.

80. LONDON BY MILFORD STAIRES.

P., B. 911.—V. III. 11.—Plate XLVIII.

[$3\frac{13}{16} \times 6\frac{13}{16}$. To border line, $3\frac{11}{16} \times 6\frac{11}{16}$].
The title, *London*, in the sky.

I. Numbered *10* just above and to the r. of the rowing-boat in l. corner. BRITISH MUSEUM.

II. This number and the parallel lines of shading in the water about it imperfectly erased.

There is probably an earlier state than I., *i. e.* before the number, but I have not seen it. I cannot be at all certain what series the *10* indicates. It is similar in shape and style to Nos. 98, 106 and 113, which are described by Vertue and Parthey as forming a series with the present example. But No. 113 is the only other of these on which I have seen a number (*3*). It seems just possible that the present etching and the example that follows, numbered *10* and *7*, might have been included in a series embracing country views of a similar shape and size, *i. e.* the six Albury views, P. 937–942 (though I have never seen these numbered), and *Hascomb Hill*, P. 950 (which is numbered *8*) and *Wiston Place*, P. 949 (which is numbered *9*). As views taken from and near Arundel House they would have a certain kinship with the views of Albury, a country seat of the Earl of Arundel.

The point from which the view is taken is shown by the house in the immediate foreground, which is also seen on the river side from the top of Arundel House in the view that follows. The jetty immediately in front is "Milford Staires' just to E. of "Arundell Staires" (see the *Bird's-eye Plan of West Central District*, No. 6 above). Only the tower of St. Paul's is seen. The view shows the N. bank of river from beyond Blackfriars to London Bridge, and in the distance London Bridge and St. Mary Overy's.

The two boats moored together in the middle of the river are the "Eel Ships" shown also in the *Long View of London*, 1647 (No. 16 above), *q. v.*

Hollar's original drawing in pen and ink for this subject is in the Pepys Library, Cambridge. It bears in the artist's hand the title "by Milford Staires." The drawing shows somewhat more of the houses on the shore on the left in front of Milford Staires, and a further figure and a boat on the shore in the l. foreground, but otherwise the etching follows it fairly closely (see Plate X).

There is an early copy of the etching (WINDSOR), probably by the same hand as those of Nos. 98, 106, 109 and 113. It measures $3\frac{11}{16} \times 6\frac{5}{8}$ (to border line).

81. LONDON FROM THE TOP OF ARUNDEL HOUSE.

P., B. 1011.—V. III. 27.—Plate XLVIII.

[$3\frac{7}{16} \times 5\frac{3}{8}$]. Signed in work, lower l.: *W. Hollar fecit.*
The title, *London from y^e top of Arundell House*, in sky above St. Paul's.
Numbered *7* to l. of margin below.

I cannot find for certain what series the *7* indicates, but compare remarks to No. 80.

The view embraces a somewhat similar distance to the preceding. Taken from a higher point it shows practically all of St. Paul's that could be seen above the houses.

On the S. of London Bridge it only shows part of St. Mary Overy's. The "Eel Ships" are again shown in the middle of the river. Part of the Inner Temple with its Hall forms the immediate background on the l. beyond Arundel House.

Borovsky refers to a state before the title and number in Windsor, but his reference was erroneously based on a copy.

82. THE COURTYARD OF ARUNDEL HOUSE: THE SOUTH SIDE.
P. 1034.—V. III. 67.—Plate XLIX.

[3¼ × 7⅝]. Signed and dated in margin lower l.: *Adam A: Bierling delin: W. Hollar* (W H in monogram) *fecit, 1646.*
The title above: *Aula Domus Arrundelianae Londini, Septentrionem versus.*

Shows a coach and six on the right, and a party of cavaliers in front of the door on the left. In the distance part of the south of the river is seen. The House as shown in the *Bird's-eye Plan of the West Central District* (No. 6 above) should be compared. This and the following are the only London views which are definitely signed by Hollar as after another master's drawings. The etching was done while Hollar was at Antwerp.

Arundel House originally belonged to the Bishops of Bath. In the reign of Edward VI it was in the hands of Lord Thomas Seymour, brother of the Protector Somerset, and after his beheadal was bought by the Earl of Arundel.

83. THE COURTYARD OF ARUNDEL HOUSE: THE NORTH SIDE.
P. 1035.—V. III. 68.—Plate XLIX.

[3³⁄₁₆ × 7⅝]. Signed and dated in margin lower r.: *Adam A: Bierling delin: W. Hollar* (W and H in monogram) *fecit 1646.*
The title above: *Aula Domus Arrundelianae Londini, Meridiem versus.*

Part of the building on the east side, with the large window, is said to have been used by Hollar as his studio. The church tower just visible to the north is that of St. Clement Danes.

84. THE SAVOY.
P. 1229.—V. III. 264.—Plate XLIX.

[2⅜ × 3⁷⁄₁₆]. Signed (in II.): *W. Hollar f :*
I. Before signature, and before rowing-boats. BRITISH MUSEUM. PEPYS LIBRARY (MAGDALENE COLLEGE, CAMBRIDGE).
II. Signature added, and two rowing-boats. BRITISH MUSEUM. GUILDHALL.

The Savoy is also shown clearly on the *Bird's-eye Plan of the West Central District of London* (No. 6 above).

A drawing by Hollar in the Pepys Library shows the Palace in the reverse direction with further buildings on either side. It may have formed the basis of the present etching

The Savoy Palace was built in 1245 by Peter, Earl of Savoy and Richmond, uncle of Eleanor, wife of Henry III. Queen Eleanor purchased it for Henry's second son, Edmund Earl of Lancaster, and it remained for some time in the possession of the Earls and Dukes of Lancaster. At the time of John of Gaunt it was burnt by Wat Tyler (1381). After remaining for over a century in ruins, it was rebuilt and endowed by Henry VII in 1505 as a Hospital of St. John the Baptist for the relief of a hundred poor people, and it continued to be used partly for this purpose until 1702, when it was finally dissolved.

For its various uses in the early eighteenth century we may quote from Strype's edition of Stow's *Survey of London*, 1720, Vol. II. (Book IV. p. 107): "This Savoy House is a very great and at this present a very ruinous building. In the midst of its buildings, is a very spacious hall. . . . This large hall is now divided into several apartments. A cooper hath a part of it for the stowing of his hoops, and for his work. Other parts of it serve for two Marshalseas for keeping prisoners, as deserters, men prest for military service, Dutch recruits, etc. . . . In this Savoy, how ruinous soever is, are divers good houses. First, the King's Printing Press for Proclamations, Acts of Parliaments, Gazets, and such like publick Papers; next a prison. Thirdly a Parish Church, and three or four other Churches and Places for Religious Assemblies; viz. for the French, for Dutch, for High Germans, and Lutherans, and lastly for the Protestant Dissenters. Here be also Harbours for many refugees, and poor people. In the year 1687 schools were set up and ordained here at the Savoy: the Masters whereof were Jesuits . . . dissolved upon the ceasing of the Government of King James. In this Savoy were placed by King William the third many families of poor French Protestants. . . ."

See also Scott's *Peveril of the Peak*, Chapter XXX. for an interesting description.

St. Mary-le-Savoy, the old Chapel of the Hospital, was destroyed by fire in 1864. In the present "Chapel Royal" (it is the property of the Crown as part of the Duchy of Lancaster) none of the old monuments, and practically nothing of the old building remain.

85. WHITEHALL FROM THE RIVER.

P. 1039.—V. III. 8.—Plate L.

The title in sky near upper margin: *Palatium Regis propè Londinum, vulgo White-hall.*
I. [$5\frac{15}{16} \times 13\frac{1}{16}$]. Before the number. Not in the British Museum.
II. The number *4* added in lower r. margin (its number in the series which includes my Nos. 22, 26, 28, 79, 86, 90, 107).
III. The plate cut down in width, showing less than $\frac{1}{2}$ in. to r. of the landing stage [$5\frac{15}{16} \times 11\frac{1}{2}$].

From its size and shape, it originally formed a set with Nos. 86, 90 and 107.

A drawing with a much more distant view of Whitehall in the same aspect, showing considerably more of the buildings on either side and the bend in the river, is in the British Museum.

Whitehall was used as the chief palace of the kings of England from the time of Henry VIII to William III. The palace belonged to Cardinal Wolsey when Archbishop of York, and its name was changed from York House (or York Place) [1] to Whitehall when handed over to the king by charter on Wolsey's disgrace. Both James I and Charles I intended to rebuild the whole palace, and designs were drawn up by Inigo Jones, but nothing was completed beyond the Banqueting House (1619–1622), the only part of the palace now remaining. The palace suffered in several fires, and was almost completely destroyed by fire in 1698, when the place was finally abandoned as a site for a royal palace.

For a full account of Whitehall and Westminster see Vol. VII. of the *London Topographical Record* (London Topographical Society), 1912.

86. PART OF WESTMINSTER, WITH PARLIAMENT HOUSE, WESTMINSTER HALL, AND THE ABBEY, FROM THE RIVER.

P. 1037.—V. III. 9.—Plate L.

Signed in work lower r. : *W. Hollar* (W and H in monogram) *fecit, 1647.*
The title in sky near upper margin : *Civitatis Westmonasteriensis pars.*
The names *Parlament House—the Hall—the Abby* above the respective buildings.
I. [$5\frac{7}{8} \times 12\frac{7}{8}$]. Before the number. Not in British Museum.
II. The number *5* added in lower r. margin (its number in the series which includes Nos. 22, 26, 28, 79, 85, 90, 107).
III. The plate cut down in width, Parliament House now being only $\frac{1}{4}$ in. from l. border line, and the Abbey $\frac{3}{8}$ in. from r. border line [$5\frac{7}{8} \times 11\frac{1}{4}$].

From its size and shape it originally formed a set with Nos. 85, 90 and 107.

87. PART OF INTERIOR OF THE HOUSE OF COMMONS DURING A SITTING.

Undescribed.

[$5\frac{1}{8} \times 3\frac{7}{8}$. The upper subject to border line, $2\frac{7}{16} \times 3\frac{11}{16}$].
A small plate with two subjects. The subject described contained in the upper part lettered: *A letter sent to Mr Pym. Mr Pym, doe not think that a guard of men can protect you, if you persist in your traiterous Courses and wiked designes. I have sent a Paper-messenger to you, and if this does not touch your heart, a dagger shall, so soon as I am recovered of my plague-sore. In the meane time you may be forborn because no better man may be endangered for you. Repent, Traitor.*

[1] Not to be confused with York House (near the present Adelphi) which also at one time belonged to the see of York, and afterward to Francis Bacon, and George Villiers, Duke of Buckingham.

I. The double plate. Occurs in John Vicars, *A Sight of the Transactions of these latter yeares* [London, 1646], on p. 17.

II. The plate divided in half. The upper part occurs in John Vicars, *True Information of the Beginning and Cause of all our Troubles.* London, 1648, on p. 15.

Not signed, but almost certainly by Hollar.

88. THE TRIAL OF ARCHBISHOP LAUD IN THE HOUSE OF LORDS.
P., B. 555.—V. II. 31 and 32.—Plate LII.

[$7\frac{7}{16}$ × $5\frac{5}{8}$]. Signed below r.: *W: Hollar fecit* (on II.).

I. With letters of reference A to I only, and before Hollar's signature. BRITISH MUSEUM. WINDSOR.

II. Signed, and reference letters K, L, M, N, T, S added. Printed on page with type. Above, title in type: *The manner and forme of the Arch-Bishops Triall in the House of Peeres*, and below: *Proverbs 11. 8. The Righteous is delivered out of Trouble, and the wicked commeth in his stead*, and references A to T.

III. Rebitten.

It occurs in this state, without descriptive type as in II., as frontispiece to W. Prynne, *Canterburies Doome:* London (printed by John Macock, for Michael Spark Senior), 1646 fol.

The walls are hung with the famous Mortlake tapestries of the time of James I, illustrating the several engagements of the British Fleet with the Spanish Armada in 1588. They were destroyed in the fire of the Houses of Parliament in 1834, but their design is preserved in a series of engravings by John Pine, published in 1739.

89. THE HOUSES OF LORDS AND COMMONS DURING SITTINGS.
P., B. 473 (part of P. 469–476).—V. I. 190, and II. 209.—Plate LIII.

Part of a plate in eight divisions (title and seven subjects with descriptive lettering). The whole plate measures $15\frac{7}{8}$ × $11\frac{7}{8}$.

There is a complete impression from the plate in the British Museum.

It generally occurs with each of the eight portions printed on separate leaves (the remaining part of the plate being in each case blocked out in the printing), and bound as a pamphlet. There are two such copies in the British Museum Library, the title (on the first portion of plate): *A Solemn League and Covenant for Reformation, and defence of Religion, the Honour and happinesse of the King, and the Peace and safety of the three kingdoms of England, Scotland and Ireland.* 1643.

The subject here described is numbered III., and is at the foot of the l. column. It measures $3\frac{9}{16}$ × $5\frac{3}{4}$ to inner border line. Text: *We shall . . . endeavour . . . to preserve the Rights . . . of the Parliaments. . . .* On the l. is shown the *House of Lords*, and on the r. the *House of Commons.*

I. Before the lettering *House of Lords* and *House of Commons.* BRITISH MUSEUM

LIBRARY, E. 253. [This copy also shows differences from II. in other sections of the plate. It is before lettering *Coristers—Singing men—Deanes—Bishops* in section II., and before *A Malignant* and *A Priest* in section IV.]
II. With the lettering. BRITISH MUSEUM and BRITISH MUSEUM LIBRARY (Grenville).

The plate is not signed, but is certainly by Hollar, both subjects and etched lettering having all the characteristics of his style.

90. NEW PALACE YARD WITH WESTMINSTER HALL, AND THE CLOCK HOUSE.

P. 1040.—V. III. 10.—Plate LI.

Signed and dated in lower r. of work : *W. Hollar* (W H in monogram) *fecit* 1647.
The title in sky near upper margin : *Sala Regalis cum Curia West-monasterij, vulgo Westminster haall.*
I. [$5\frac{13}{16} \times 12\frac{15}{16}$]. Before the number. Not in the British Museum.
II. The number *6* added in lower r. margin (its order in series which includes my Nos. 22, 26, 28, 79, 85, 86, 107).
III. The plate cut down in width, the subject now only extending $\frac{1}{4}$ in. beyond the clock tower on the r. [$5\frac{13}{16} \times 11\frac{1}{4}$].

From its size and shape it originally formed a set with Nos. 85, 86 and 107.

91. WESTMINSTER HALL. INTERIOR, WITH THE TRIAL OF THE EARL OF STRAFFORD. 1641.

P., B. 551.—V. II. 33.—Plate LIII.

[$9\frac{15}{16} \times 10\frac{15}{16}$]. Signed in work lower l. : *W. Hollar fecit.*
I. (On same plate as No. 23 above). Described by Parthey as in the collection of Francis Graves, London. I have not seen an impression.
II. The plate divided, separating the present subject from No. 23. The title along the top : *The True Maner of the Sitting of the Lords and Commons of both Howses of Parliament, upon the tryal of Thomas Earle of Strafford, Lord Lieutenant of Ireland,* 1641. Reference letters and Index of personages (by office and title) in the margin below.
III. The English title replaced by the German : *Abbildung der Session des Parlaments. . . .*
IV. Above the German title is added main title in Latin : *Parlamentum Londinense.*

92. WESTMINSTER AND WHITEHALL FROM THE RIVER.

The background in the oval portrait of Charles I, 1649, after Van Dyck (P., B. 1432.— V. III. 50).

93. PART OF WESTMINSTER WITH PARLIAMENT HOUSE FROM THE THAMES.

[5⅛ × 3⅞. The upper part to border line, 2½ × 3¹¹⁄₁₆]. A small plate with two historical subjects. The view described contained in the upper subject lettered: *The Citie Trained Bands, and the brave Sea-men with Barges and Long-boates adorn'd with streamers drums and trumpets, and furnisht with Ship-guns and other Warrlike instruments, guard the Lords and Commons safely to Parl: by land and water.*
Occurs in John Vicars, *A Sight of the Transactions of these latter yeares.* [London, 1646], p. 19.

Not signed, but almost certainly by Hollar.

94. WESTMINSTER WITH PARLIAMENT HOUSE FROM THE RIVER.

The background of P., B. 611, V. XIII. 21 (*Summer*, from the three-quarter length *Seasons*).

95. WHITEHALL (THE BANQUETING HALL), FROM ST. JAMES'S PARK.

P. 1442.—Plate II.

The background in portrait of Charles II, 1649 (P. 1442).

96. WHITEHALL (THE BANQUETING HALL), FROM ST. JAMES'S PARK.

The background in the oval portrait of Charles II (P. 1443).

97. ST. JAMES'S PARK, WITH WHITEHALL AND ST. PAUL'S IN THE DISTANCE.

The background of P. 607 (*Summer*, from the full-length *Seasons*, P. 606–609).

98. WHITEHALL FROM THE RIVER, WITH LAMBETH IN THE DISTANCE.

P. 912.—V. III. 12.—Plate LVII.

[3¹¹⁄₁₆ × 6¾. To border line, 3⁹⁄₁₆ × 6⅝].
Lettered *White Hall, Lambeth*, and on the river l., *Thames flu:*

Similar in shape and style to Nos. 80, 106 and 113, the four being described by Vertue and Parthey as forming a series.

There is a good early copy without the inscription *Thames flu:* [3⁹⁄₁₆ × 6½, to border-line]. It is probably by the same hand as the copies of Nos. 80, 106, 109 and 113.

99. WESTMINSTER ABBEY. EXTERIOR: NORTH.

P. 1041.—V. IX. 23.—Plate LIV.

[$8\frac{9}{16}$ × $12\frac{3}{4}$].   Signed and dated in lower r.: *W. Hollar fecit: 1654.*

I. With Latin title in upper r.: *Westmonast: ecclesiæ conv: facies aquilonalis.*
Cartouche upper l. with name of donor of plate, William Bromley.   Before the number.
This state shows the lines of ruling about the title and donor's name more clearly
than the following.

WINDSOR.   BRITISH MUSEUM LIBRARY (in King's Library copy of Dodsworth and
Dugdale, *Monasticon*, I. (1655), between pp. 56 and 57).

II. The number *56* added in lower r.   Intended in this state for Dodsworth and
Dugdale, *Monasticon*, I. (1655), at p. 56 (as in the copy in WINDSOR).
BRITISH MUSEUM LIBRARY (in Daniel King, *The Cathedrall and Conventuall Churches of
England and Wales*, 1656).

III. English title added beneath the Latin: *The North Prospect of the Conventuall
Church of Westmynster.*   The number altered to *18*.   Possibly intended in this state for
D. King's series, *The Cathedrall and Conventuall Churches of England and Wales*, 1656.
BRITISH MUSEUM (two impressions: the one in the Crace collection having the
18 altered in MS. to *56*).   It also occurs in this state in Dodsworth and Dugdale,
Monasticon, I. (1682), between pp. 56 and 57 (in the King's Library copy, the number is
hidden in the binding).

The order of states in Nos. 99 and 100 is extremely puzzling.   The fact that
impressions get inserted in books in states not originally intended for the respective
publications confuses comparison.   There were, no doubt, issues of Vol. I. of the
Monasticon Anglicanum, with original date 1655 on title page, later than 1656, the year
in which Daniel King's series of plates, *The Cathedrall and Conventuall Churches of
England and Wales*, was published.   And the British Museum Library copy of the latter
contains plates with page numbers as intended for the *Monasticon*.   After the alteration
of the *Monasticon* page numbers to *17* and *18* (the numbers for King's series?), later
impressions of the plates inserted in the *Monasticon* merely have the *17* and *18* corrected
in MS.

Two other plates illustrating Westminster in King's series were etched by Daniel
King himself, *i.e.* the *Ground Plan* (after Newcourt), and a *South View of Westminster
Abbey*.   Both of these also appeared in the *Monasticon* (numbered *54* and *58* respectively).
The latter also occurs with number *19* (probably as intended for King's publication,
though the British Museum Library series shows both plates with numbers as in the
Monasticon.   It occurs in this state, the *19* altered in MS. to *59* in the *Monasticon*,
Vol. I. ed. 1682, between pp. 58 and 59).

King was an amateur of Chester, who based his style on Hollar.   Dugdale is said
to have called him an ignorant, silly knave (see Redgrave, *Dictionary of Artists*).
Besides the plates for the *Monasticon*, and his own *Cathedrall and Conventuall Churches*,
King's most important work is his *Vale-Royal of England, or the County Palatine of
Chester*.   London, 1656.

100. WESTMINSTER ABBEY. EXTERIOR: WEST.

P. 1042.—V. IX. 22.—Plate LV.

[9¹³⁄₁₆ × 6¾].

I. With Latin title in centre above: *Westmonasteriensis Ecclesiae, (quondā Conventualis), facies occidentalis.*

And in cartouche upper r.: *P.S. Ne memoria Petri, Pauli modo cum mole ruat. P. Wenceslaus Hollar E: Bohem.*

Before the number, and before brackets in lettering on cartouche.

WINDSOR. GUILDHALL (both the preceding with brackets as in II. added in MS.). BRITISH MUSEUM.

II. The number *60* added in lower r. Brackets added enclosing (*Pauli modo*) in lettering in the cartouche.

Intended in this state for Dodsworth and Dugdale, *Monasticon*, I. (1655), at p. 60 (*e.g.* in the Windsor copy).

BRITISH MUSEUM LIBRARY (in D. King, *The Cathedrall and Conventuall Churches of England and Wales*, 1656).

III. English title added beneath the Latin: *The West Prospect of the late Conventuall Church of Westminster.* The number altered to *17.* Possibly intended in this state for D. King, *The Cathedrall and Conventuall Churches of England and Wales*, 1656.

BRITISH MUSEUM LIBRARY (in Dodsworth and Dugdale, *Monasticon*, I. (1655), between pp. 56 and 57, and in *Monasticon*, I. (1682), between pp. 60 and 61, *60* being added in MS. over the engraved *17* in each edition).

101. THE CORONATION OF CHARLES II IN WESTMINSTER ABBEY.

P. 575.—Plate LVI.

[15 × 19¼; including clear margin below of ¹¹⁄₁₆ in.]. Without signature or lettering.

Occurs, folded, in John Ogilby, *The Entertainment of his most Excellent Majestie Charles II in his Passage through . . . London to his Coronation.* London (T. Roycroft). 1662. The second part of the book (after p. [166]) has the title: *A Brief Narrative of his Majestie's Solemn Coronation: with his Magnificent Proceeding, and Royal Feast in Westminster-Hall,* and the Plate in BRITISH MUSEUM (King's Library) copy, precedes this second title.

102. WESTMINSTER ABBEY. THE TOMB OF HENRY VII.

P. 2303.—V. IX. 156.—Plate LIV.

[11¾ × 14⅝]. Signed in centre of lower margin: *W: Hollar fecit aqua forti A⁰ 1665, Aetat: 58 compl:*

With dedication to Gilbert Sheldon, Archbishop of Canterbury.

I. In upper l. the page number 442. Occurs, folded, between pp. 442 and 443, in Francis Sandford, *Genealogical History of the Kings of England.* London, 1677, fol.

II. The page number changed to *472.* Plate much worn and reworked. Occurs, folded, between pp. 472 and 473 in Sandford, *Genealogical History*, 2nd edition, 1707, fol.

103. WESTMINSTER ABBEY. TOMB OF AVELINA, COUNTESS OF LANCASTER.

P. 2312.—V. IX. 205, and 216.

[$11\frac{1}{4} \times 7\frac{3}{8}$]. Signed on r. below: *W. Hollar* (W and H in monogram) *fecit 1666*.
I. Before lettering. (Proof described by Vertue, IX. 205.)
II. In upper l. the page number *104*. With dedication to Sir Thomas Clifford. Occurs on p. 104 in Sandford, *Genealogical History of England*, 1677.
III. Worn and reworked. On p. 104 of Sandford, 2nd edition, 1707.

Avelina (first wife of Edmund Earl of Lancaster), † 1269.

104. WESTMINSTER ABBEY. TOMB OF EDMUND EARL OF LANCASTER.

P. 2313.—V. IX. 217.

[$12\frac{5}{8} \times 7\frac{1}{2}$].
With dedication to Charles, Earl of Carlisle.
In upper l. the page number, *106*. Occurs on p. 106 of Sandford, *Genealogical History of England*, 1677, and 2nd edition, 1707.

Edmund Earl of Lancaster, † 1296.

105. WESTMINSTER ABBEY. TOMB OF PHILIPPA, DUCHESS OF YORK.

P. 2379.—V. IX. 218.

[$8\frac{13}{16} \times 7\frac{1}{8}$].
With dedication to Philip Earl of Pembroke.
I. In upper l. the page number, *364*. Occurs on p. 364 of Sandford, *Genealogical History of England*, 1677.
II. The page number changed to *382*. On p. 382 of Sandford, 2nd edition, 1707.

Philippa, daughter of John Mohun, and wife of Edward Duke of York, † 1433

WESTMINSTER AND TOTHILL FIELDS FROM THE RIVER.
At the foot of Sheet 1 of the *Long Bird's-eye View of London from Bankside*, 1647 (No. 16 above), *q. v.*

106. TOTHILL FIELDS.

P. 913.—V. III. 13.—Plate LVII.

[$3\frac{11}{16} \times 6\frac{3}{4}$. To border line, $3\frac{9}{16} \times 6\frac{5}{8}$].
Title in centre above: *Tootehill fields*.
In the background are Westminster Abbey (lettered *St Peter in Westminster*) and St. Paul's (lettered *St Paul in London*).

Similar in shape and style to Nos. 80, 98 and 113, and described by Vertue and Parthey as forming with these a series of four.

There is an early copy which reads *S. Peter . . .* and *S. Paul . . .* in place of *St Peter . . .* and *St Paul.* It is probably by the same hand as the copies of Nos. 80, 98, 109 and 113.

107. LAMBETH PALACE.

P. 1038.—V. III. 7.—Plate LI.

[5$\frac{15}{16}$ × 12$\frac{15}{16}$]. Signed in the work l. below: *W. Hollar* (W and H in monogram) *fecit 1647.*
The title above: *Palatium Archiepiscopi Cantuariensis propae Londinum, vulgo Lambeth House.*
I. Before the number. Not in the British Museum.
II. The number *3* added in lower r. margin (its order in the series which includes Nos. 22, 26, 28, 79, 85, 86 and 90).
III. The plate cut down slightly on either side, the sailing barge being only $\frac{1}{4}$ in. from l. margin [5$\frac{15}{16}$ × 11$\frac{3}{8}$].

From its size and shape, it originally formed a set with Nos. 85, 86 and 90.

108. PART OF LAMBETH PALACE WITH A VIEW ACROSS TO THE NORTH SIDE OF THE THAMES.

Undescribed.

[5 × 3$\frac{13}{16}$. The lower subject to border line: 2$\frac{3}{8}$ × 3$\frac{11}{16}$].
A small plate with two historical subjects. The view described contained in the lower subject lettered: *The Rising of Prentices and Sea-men on Southwark side to assault the Archbishops of Canterburys House at Lambeth.*
Occurs in John Vicar's (1) *A Sight of the Transactions of these latter yeares* [London, 1646]; (2) *True Information of the Beginning and Cause of all our Troubles:* London, 1648; (3) Ditto: London, 1648 (1649 according to present calendar); on p. 5 in each.

Not signed, but certainly by Hollar.

D (109–132)

RICHMOND AND WINDSOR

109. RICHMOND.

P. 1058.—V. III. 23.—Plate LVIII.

[4$\frac{5}{8}$ × 13$\frac{1}{2}$]. Signed, in the work towards r. below: *W. Hollar, fecit 1638.*
The title in centre of sky: *Richmond.*

There is an early and most deceptive copy of nearly the same size [4$\frac{7}{16}$ × 13$\frac{1}{8}$] and in same direction (BRITISH MUSEUM and WINDSOR). The Durrant Sale Catalogue

G

(1856) contained a copy described as by Van der Gucht, and Parthey in the *Nachträge* to his catalogue refers to a copy in the same direction as the original as by Michael van der Gucht. They both probably refer to the copy of which there are impressions in the British Museum, and at Windsor. I do not know on what basis the attribution to Michael van der Gucht is founded. If by a Van der Gucht at all, one would be more inclined to think of Michael's son Gerard Van der Gucht. It is worth noting in this relation that the copy shows a B on the ship's flag, which bears a blank shield surmounted by a crown in the original. Other signs of the original are full stop after *Richmond.* in the title, and a comma after *Hollar,* in the signature. Also the Prince of Wales's Feathers shown on the canopy of the barge in three places in the original lose all distinctive form in the copy. Finally, the wheel on the quay on extreme left is that of a crane ; the cogs being omitted in the copy. The copy is probably by the same hand as those of Nos. 80, 98, 106, 113.

The decoration of the barge with the Prince of Wales's Feathers makes it certain that Prince Charles is intended in one of the boys in the front of the group. One would naturally expect him to be the only figure wearing a hat, but from the position of the group and size of the figures, it is most likely that Prince Charles is shown in the taller of the two boys to the right of the group, and his younger brother, James Duke of York, the smaller boy in the hat. The little girl further back might be the Princess Mary.

A drawing in the British Museum shows the Palace from a similar point of view, but does not extend so far at either side. But it was probably used as a study for the etching. There is also an attractive drawing by Hollar of Richmond (an entirely different view) in the Royal Library, Windsor. It has been reproduced in an outline etching, attributed in the same collection to Van der Gucht.

Richmond Palace was one of the favourite royal residences from the time of Edward III to Elizabeth. An old manor seems to have been originally enlarged for use as a palace by Edward III, and retained its old name of Sheen, until the time of Henry VII, who rebuilt it after a fire, between 1497–1501. He rechristened it Richmond after his earldom of Richmond in Yorkshire. Wolsey received permission to reside at the Royal Manor of Richmond after his gift of Hampton Court to the King ; but apart from Wolsey it seems to have been exclusively used by the Royal Family until the death of Elizabeth. It was favoured less by the Stuarts, but Prince Henry lived here a considerable part of the years 1604–1612, and Charles Prince of Wales as well. About 1626 the Palace and Manor were given by the King to Queen Henrietta Maria, who lived here with the Royal children.

The building suffered considerably during the Commonwealth, and though restored to Henrietta Maria in 1660, and granted later to James Duke of York, it was apparently never properly restored, and finally in 1703 what remained was for the most part broken up. A small portion of the old Palace still in existence, with the old gateway facing Richmond Green. It is Crown property, occupied as a private residence.

110. MAP OF BERKSHIRE.

P. 659.

[$7\frac{3}{8}$ × $12\frac{3}{16}$]. Signed lower r.: *W. Hollar fec: 1671.*
Title in cartouche in centre above: *A Mapp of Barkshire with its Hundreds by Rich: Blome, by his Maj^{ties} especiall Command A° 1671.*
Arms, and Dedication in upper l.: *To y^e R^t Worshipfull Sr Thomas Delman of Shaw in this County of Enderbe in Leicestershire and of Thornton in Warwickshire K^t This Mapp is humbly Dedicated by Ric Blome.*
Occurs folded at p. 38 of R. Blome, *Brittania,* 1673, fol.

111. A SMALLER MAP OF BERKSHIRE.

P. 660.—V. III. 313.

[$7\frac{5}{16}$×$9\frac{3}{8}$]. Signed below r.: *W. Hollar fecit.*
[Title in cartouche upper l.: *A Mapp of Barkshire with its Hundreds.*
Scale of miles in centre below. Below on l.: *London Printed for Rich: Blome 1671.*
II (?). As described. In *Speed's Maps Epitomiz'd:* London, 1681.
III. The number *2* added in upper r. In Tho. Taylor, *England exactly Described* [London, 1715].
IV. *Printed and sold by Tho: Taylor at ye Golden Lyon in Fleet Street* in place of *Printed for Rich: Blome 1671.* In Tho: Taylor, *England exactly Described* [1716?]
V. *Printed and sold by Tho: Bakewell.* WINDSOR.

There was evidently an earlier issue than the one which appeared in *Speed's Maps Epitomiz'd,* 1681, and I have consequently described the above as 2nd state with a query. There may, of course, have been no difference in the early state. Compare Nos. 1, 2 and 3.

112. MAP OF BERKSHIRE WITH A VIEW OF WINDSOR CASTLE FROM THE SOUTH.

P. 658.—V. III. 307.—Plate LVIII (the upper part of print, state III).

[$14\frac{5}{8}$ × $19\frac{7}{8}$]. Signed towards l. below: *W. Hollar fecit 1666.*
The title in the centre of the map above: *A New Mapp of Barkshire with all the Hundreds Parkes and other Places thereunto belonging.*
Along the top is the view of *Ye South side of Windsor Castle,* flanked by two costume studies of a *Knight of the Garter.*
I. The publisher's address in rectangle below r.: *London, Sould with all other Countey and Countrey Maps by John Overton, at ye White Horse in Giltspur Street, between Newgate and Pey Corner.* WINDSOR.
II. The address altered to . . . *at ye White Horse without Newgate neere the Fountaine tavern.* BRITISH MUSEUM.
Occurs in Ashmole, *Antiquities of Berkshire,* 1719, Vol. I. p. 1 (*e.g.* in copy at Windsor; not in British Museum copies of Ashmole in any edition).

III. The plate cut, dividing the upper strip with view from the map. The view has been reworked, *e. g.* on the wall below St. George's Chapel. BRITISH MUSEUM.

In WINDSOR the 1736 edition of Ashmole, *Antiquities of Berkshire*, contains the view in this state inset on an impression of the map in same state as II.

113. WINDSOR CASTLE FROM THE SOUTH-EAST.

P., B. 914.—V. III. 14.—Plate LIX.

[$3\frac{11}{16} \times 6\frac{5}{8}$. To border line, $3\frac{9}{16} \times 6\frac{1}{2}$]. Signed and dated in work, lower l.: *W. Hollar fecit 1644.*

The title, *Windsor*, in the sky.

I. Before the number.

II. The number *3* added in lower r., a small corner of the shading being cleared away for it. GUILDHALL.

Similar in shape and style to Nos. 80, 98 and 106, and described by Vertue and Parthey as forming a series with these. No. 80 is the only other print of the four which bears a number (*10*), and then not in any relation to a series of four. The *3* may indicate relation to another set, which I have not identified.

There is a deceptive early copy without the signature, probably by the same hand as the copies of Nos. 80, 98, 106 and 109. It measures $3\frac{1}{2} \times 6\frac{1}{2}$ in. to border line.

114. WINDSOR CASTLE. TWO VIEWS, ONE ABOVE THE OTHER.

P. 1072.—V. III. 265.—Plate LIX.

[$12\frac{1}{4} \times 14\frac{7}{8}$]. Signed in lower r.: *W. Hollar delineavit et sculpsit.*

The upper view with title: *Prospect of the Castle from the S.E.*

The lower view is a bird's-eye taken from nearly the same quarter. The main title *Windsor Castle* and references 1–28 in compartment upper r. of the bird's-eye view.

In margin lower l.: *Pag. 131.* Occurs in Elias Ashmole, *Institution . . . of the . . . Order of the Garter:* London, 1672, and 1693, folded, as p. 131.

115. WINDSOR CASTLE. THREE VIEWS, ONE ABOVE ANOTHER.

P. 1073.—V. III. 267.

[$12\frac{1}{8} \times 15\frac{1}{8}$]. Signed in work in lower l. foreground: *W. Hollar delin: & sculp.*

Three titles (*a*) To top view: *Prospect of Windsor Castle & Towne from South S. West;* (*b*) To middle view: *Prospect of the same Castle from West South West;* (*c*) To bottom view: *Prospect of it from West & by South.*

In lower margin: *Pag. 132.* Occurs in Ashmole, *Garter*, 1672, and 1693, folded, as p. 132.

116. WINDSOR CASTLE, FROM THE NORTH.

P. 1074.—V. III. 266.—Plate LVIII.

[7⅝ × 14⅛]. Signed in margin lower r.: *W. Hollar fecit 1667.*
In lower l. margin the signature of draughtsman: *Christoph^r Wren delineavit.*
The title on a scroll along the top: *Prospect of Windsor Castle from the North.*
In lower l. margin: p. 134. Occurs in Ashmole, *Garter*, 1672, and 1693, folded, as
p. 134.

One of the few of Hollar's etchings described in this volume after another artist,
and of particular interest as based on a drawing by the famous architect Sir Christopher
Wren.

117. WINDSOR CASTLE, FROM THE NORTH.

Forms the background of part of the plate (P. 580.—V. VII. 232) entitled *A
Proceeding of the Soveraigne & Knights Companions at the Feast of St George, designed
by Marcus Gerard, and set forth in the 20 yeare of Queene Elizabeth, by Thomas Dawes,
sometime Rougecroix Pursu^t at Arm^es*, which is signed *Marcus Gerard inv.*, and *W. Hollar
fecit 1666.*
In lower l. margin: *Pag: 515.* It occurs in Ashmole, *Garter*, 1672, and 1693, folded,
between pp. 514 and 515.

In this plate Hollar reproduces on a smaller scale in four strips an extremely rare
etching in nine sheets, by Marcus Gheraerts the elder (1576). The only perfect set of
impressions of the original is in the British Museum. The set in the Heralds' College
is mutilated. It is not signed, and Hollar's copy is the authority for the original
authorship.

WINDSOR CASTLE, FROM THE SOUTH.

Plate LVIII.

Part of the *Map of Berkshire*, No. 112, *q. v.*

118. ST. GEORGE'S CHAPEL, WINDSOR CASTLE. EXTERIOR ELEVA-
TION FROM SOUTH, AND GROUND PLAN.

P. 1075.—V. IX. 150.

[10⅓ × 14¾]. Signed in centre below: *Wenceslaus Hollar delineavit et sculpsit.*
The upper part with title: *The Prospect of St. George's Chapell from the South*, and
further r. *The Tomb House.*
The lower part with title: *The Ground-plot of St. George's Chapell.*
I. Before all inscriptions, except signature and scale of feet. WINDSOR.
II. With inscriptions as above, and in lower l.: *Page 137.* Occurs in Ashmole, *Garter*,
1672, and 1693, folded as pp. 137, 138 (between pp. 136 and 149).

This view is merely an elevation of the chapel with clear sky and ground and no buildings at side. The point of view is slightly higher than in No. 119, and more of the roof is in consequence visible.

119. ST. GEORGE'S CHAPEL, WINDSOR CASTLE. EXTERIOR FROM SOUTH, AND GROUND PLAN.

P. 1076.—V. IX. 151.—Plate LX.

[11⅝ × 13⅞, to border line]. Signed in lower r.: *W. Hollar delineavit.*
The upper part with title on cartouche: *Capellae Regiae ac Collegiatae S. Georgii in Castro de Windsore a Meridie Prospectus.*
Below the title on an extension of the same cartouche the inscription of the donors of the plate: *In piorum olim Fundatorum[e] memoriam Decanus et Canonici praeclarae hujus Capellae hoc posuere A° 1671.*
The lower part with title: *Areae ejusdem Capellae Ichnographia.*
In lower l. the page number *87*. Occurs in Dugdale, *Monasticon*, Vol. III. (1673), Pt. 2 (*Ecclesiae Collegiatae*), between pp. 86 and 87.

Very similar to the preceding, but with a more definitely picturesque intention as a view. Clouds are shown in the sky, the ground is shaded, and other castle buildings are shown between the ends of the chapel and the margin of print.

Only signed as *drawn* by Hollar, but there seems every reason to think the etching is his also.

120. ST. GEORGE'S CHAPEL, WINDSOR CASTLE. EXTERIOR, WEST.

P. 1077.—V. IX. 152.

[11⅞ × 8¾]. Signed on shaded ground in centre below: *W. Hollar delin: et sculp:*
Below in the margin the title: *Prospect of the West End of St Georg's Chapell.*
In lower l. margin, *Pag: 139.*
I. With signature, but before title and page number. WINDSOR.
II. As described. Occurs in Ashmole, *Garter*, 1672, and 1693, as p. 139 (between pp. 136 and 149).

121. ST. GEORGE'S CHAPEL, WINDSOR CASTLE. INTERIOR: THE NAVE.

P. 1080.—V. IX. 146.—Plate LXI.

[14⅞ × 11⅞].
Title in lower margin: *Prospect of the Inside of the Chapel,* and references to numbers on the plates 1–8.
In lower l. *Pag: 140.*
I. Before title and reference and page numbers. BRITISH MUSEUM. WINDSOR.
II. As described above. Occurs in Ashmole, *Garter*, 1672, and 1693, folded as p. 140 (between pp. 136 and 149).

122. ST. GEORGE'S CHAPEL, WINDSOR CASTLE. INTERIOR: THE TRANSEPT, LOOKING SOUTH.

P. 1082.—V. IX. 147.

[11¾ × 8¼]. Signed in lower l.: *W. Hollar delin: et sculp: 1663.*
In the margin are references to numbers 1–8 on the subject.
In lower l. *Pag: 142.*
I. Before letters, except signature. WINDSOR.
II. As described above. Occurs in Ashmole, *Garter*, 1672, and 1693, as p. 142 (between pp. 136 and 149).

123. ST. GEORGE'S CHAPEL, WINDSOR CASTLE. THE CHOIR-SCREEN AND ORGAN, FROM THE WEST.

P. 1083.—V. IX. 148.

[7⅕₆ × 9⅝]. Signed in centre below: *W. Hollar sculp.*
Title above: *Prospect of the Cancell, or Screen from the West.*
References below to numbers 1–3 on the subject.
Below on l.: *Pag: 144.* Occurs in Ashmole, *Garter*, 1672, and 1693, on same folding plate as No. 124, as p. 144 (between pp. 136 and 149).

124. ST. GEORGE'S CHAPEL, WINDSOR CASTLE. THE CHOIR, WITH SCREEN AND ORGAN, FROM THE EAST.

P. 1084.—V. IX. 149.—Plate LXIII.

[7¼ × 11¼]. Signed r. below: *W. Hollar delin. et sculp.*
The title in compartment in centre above: *Prospect of the Cancell from the East.*
Below, references to numbers 1–5 on the subject.
Below l.: *pag 145.*
I. Before all lettering, and before compartment above. WINDSOR. BRITISH MUSEUM.
II. Compartment cleared above for the title. BRITISH MUSEUM.
III. Title and other lettering added as described above. Occurs in Ashmole, *Garter*, 1672, and 1693 (on same folding plate as No. 123), as p. 145 (between pp. 136 and 149).

125. ST. GEORGE'S CHAPEL, WINDSOR CASTLE. INTERIOR: THE CHOIR, FROM THE WEST.

P. 1078.—V. IX. 144.—Plate LXII.

[11⅕₆ × 12⅕₆].
I. Before title and other lettering; but signed near centre below on the pavement: *W. Hollar delin: et sculp. 1663.* WINDSOR.
II. The signature in I. erased. Now signed in lower margin r.: *W. Hollar Scenographus Regis delineavit et sculpsit.*
Compartment added in centre above with title: *Prospect of the Choire from the West.*
In the lower margin references and Nos. 1–12. Left: *Pag. 146.* Occurs in Ashmole, *Garter*, 1672, and 1693, folded, as p. 146 (between pp. 136 and 149). The plate shows considerable signs of wear in the second edition.

126. ST. GEORGE'S CHAPEL, WINDSOR CASTLE. INTERIOR: THE CHOIR, FROM THE WEST. A SECOND PLATE.

P. 1081.—V. IX. 199.

[7⅞ × 12¼]. Signed in centre of margin below: *Wenceslaus Hollar delineavit et sculpsit, 1660.*

WINDSOR. BRITISH MUSEUM.

Similar to No. 125, but not so high.

Parthey (*Nachträge*) seems to have misread the Durrant sale Catalogue, 1856, No. 31, and makes an early state before the compartment above (which in the Durrant Catalogue refers to No. 127 only).

127. ST. GEORGE'S CHAPEL, WINDSOR CASTLE. INTERIOR: CHOIR, FROM THE EAST.

P. 1079.—V. IX. 145.

[10⅝ × 13¼].

I. Before title, and the lettering, but signed immediately below the margin of work lower r.: *W. Hollar delineavit et sculpsit, 1663.* WINDSOR.

II. The signature in I. erased. Now signed rather lower r.: *W. Hollar Scenographus Regis delineavit et sculpsit.* Compartment added in centre above with title: *Prospect of the Choire from the East.*

In the lower margin references and Nos. 1–8. Left: *Pag: 147.* Occurs in Ashmole, *Garter*, 1672, and 1693, folded, as p. 147 (between pp. 136 and 149).

128. ST. GEORGE'S CHAPEL, WINDSOR CASTLE. TOMB OF EDWARD IV.

P. 2282.—V. IX. 210.

[11¹⁵⁄₁₆ × 12⅞].

In upper l. the page number *390*. Occurs folded in Sandford, *Genealogical History,* 1677, between pp. 390 and 391, and in the 2nd edition, 1707, between pp. 412 and 413.

Not signed, but the etching certainly by Hollar.

The engraved inscription and coat of arms added by another hand. Parthey suggests that it was Hollar's last work.

129. ST. GEORGE'S CHAPEL, WINDSOR CASTLE. TOMB OF CHARLES SOMERSET, EARL OF WORCESTER, AND ELIZABETH HIS WIFE.

P. 2363.—V. IX. 209.

[8¾ × 8¼]. Signed l. below: W. Hollar (W and H in monogram) *fecit 1666.*

I. In upper r. the page number *329*. Occurs in Sandford, *Genealogical History,* 1677, on p. 329.

II. The page number changed to 339. On p. 339, in Sandford, 2nd edition, 1707.

130. ST. GEORGE'S CHAPEL, WINDSOR CASTLE. MONUMENTAL BRASS OF ANNE DUCHESS OF EXETER, AND THOMAS ST. LEOGER (SENT-LYNGER), HER SECOND HUSBAND.

P. 2414.—V. IX. 212.

[6½ × 5⅞]. Signed l. below: *W. Hollar fecit 1667.*

I. The page number 377 towards r. above. Occurs in Sandford, *Genealogical History*, 1677, on p. 377.

II. The page number changed to 396. On p. 396 of Sandford, 2nd edition, 1707.

Anne Duchess of Exeter, was sister of King Edward IV.

131. A STATE BANQUET IN ST. GEORGE'S HALL, WINDSOR CASTLE.

P., B. 1581.—V. II. 48.—Plate LXIV.

[11⅞ × 14⅞].

I. Before letters. BRITISH MUSEUM. WINDSOR.

II. Compartment added in centre above with title: *The Prospect of the inside of St. George's Hall.*

In margin below references and Nos. 1–13, and l.: *Pag: 593.* Occurs in Ashmole, *Garter*, 1672, and 1693, between pp. 592 and 593. The plate is considerably worn in the second edition.

132. ETON COLLEGE CHAPEL. EXTERIOR, FROM THE NORTH.

P. 972.—V. III. 425, and IX. 219.—Plate LXIII.

[10⅛ × 14¾]. Signed in lower margin towards l.: *W. Hollar delineavit et sculpsit, 1672.*

Title in cartouche above r.: *Capellae Collegii Regalis de Eton ab Aquilone Prospectus.*

I. Before page number. WINDSOR.

II. In margin lower l.: *P. 195.* Occurs folded in Dugdale, *Monasticon*, Vol. III. (1673) Pt. 2, between pp. 194 and 195.

ETCHINGS ISSUED IN SERIES.

As the catalogue is arranged according to locality, I add here a list of the London views which make sets.

Nos. 26, 79, 28, 22, form a natural set from their size, and are included in a single numeration 1–8 in their late states with Nos. 107, 85, 86 and 90, which are the longer London views.

Then Nos. 80, 98, 106 and 113 are of the same size, and described by Vertue and Parthey as a series, but even their late states show no numeration to associate them like the eight preceding (No. 80 is numbered *10,* and No. 113, *3*).

No. 81 is numbered *7*, but I cannot be certain what series this indicates (see notes in the catalogue).

Finally the six Islington views (Nos. *72–77*) unquestionably form a series, but are not numbered.

CORRESPONDENCE OF NUMBERS

IN PARTHEY'S CATALOGUE, AND IN THE PRESENT VOLUME.

(The numbers prefixed with B are from Borovsky.)

Parthey	Hind	Parthey	Hind	Parthey	Hind
473	89	1005	13	1072	114
530	69	1006	12	1073	115
551	91	1007	14	1074	116
552	23	1008	Not by Hollar	1075	118
555	88	1009	Not by Hollar	1076	119
575	101	1010	Not by Hollar	1077	120
580	117		(It is the upper part	1078	125
581	131		of the "Table of	1079	127
607	97		Hollar's Works" in	1080	121
609	30		Vertue's *Description*	1081	126
611	94		*of the Works of*	1082	122
648	7		*Hollar*, 1745, and	1083	123
658	112		1759.)	1084	124
659	110	1011	81	1229	84
660	111	1012	17	1432	92
B 661, *b*	1	1013	18	1442	95
663	4	1014	16	1443	96
664	5	1015	19	2236	51
667	2	1016	36	2242	60
B 668, *a*	3	1017	35	2248	48
671	1	1018	37	2255	63
907	28	1019	38	2264	61
908	22	1020	39	2277	50
909	79	1021	40	2282	128
910	26	1022	41	2286	67
911	80	1023	34	2290	49
912	98	1024	44	2292	58
913	106	1025	42	2301	62
914	113	1026	45	2303	102
915	72	1027	46	2309	47
916	73	1028	68	2311	56
917	74	1029	32	2312	103
918	/5	1030	33	2313	104
919	76	1031	70	2319	64
920	77	1032	21	2320	54
972	132	1033	27	2321	66
977	20	1034	82	2322	52
979	71	1035	83	2336	57
999	7 (*a*)	1036	29	2341	59
999, *a* (Nachträge)	15	1037	86	2361	55
1000	8	1038	107	2363	129
1001	9	1039	85	2375	65
1002	6	1040	90	2377	53
1003	10	1041	99	2379	105
1004	11	1042	100	2414	130
		1058	109	2687	68

INDEX TO THE CATALOGUE

PLATE I

Serenissimus Princeps, Carolus D:G: Angliæ,
Scotiæ, & Hiberniæ, REX, etc. ∞

Ant: van Dyck, pinxit.   W: Hollar fecit, 1649

PORTRAIT OF CHARLES I, WITH BACKGROUND OF WESTMINSTER AND WHITEHALL. 92.

PLATE II

CAROLVS II. D.G. MAGNÆ BRITTANIÆ FRAN. et HIBERNIÆ REX.

Hanc Maiestatis suæ Effigiem ab Antonio van Dycke Equite sic depictam, Humillimus Cliens Wenceslaus Hollar Boh.
v Aqua forti ari insculpsit. Dedicauit Consecrauit, Anno 1649.

Ant van Dycke pinxit. W. Hollar fecit. et exc.

PORTRAIT OF CHARLES II, WITH WHITEHALL (THE BANQUETING HALL) IN THE BACKGROUND. 95

PLATE III

CAPTAIN KEMPTHORN'S ENGAGEMENT IN THE "MARY ROSE" WITH SEVEN ALGERINE MEN-OF-WAR. P. 1247.

PLATE IV

A SHELL. P. 2200.

MUFFS AND OTHER ARTICLES OF DRESS AND TOILET. P. 1951.

PLATE V

IGNATII IONES MAG: BRIT: ARCHITECTI GE-NERALIS, VERA EFFIGIES,

Anth: van Dycke Eques pinxit

W: Hollar fecit 1649.

PORTRAIT OF INIGO JONES. AFTER VAN DYCK. P. 1428.

GULIELMUS DUGDALE
Ætatis. 50. A. MDCLVI.

OVID.
Nescire qua natale solum dulcedine cunctos
Ducit, et immemores non sinit esse sui.

PORTRAIT OF WILLIAM DUGDALE. P. 1392.

PLATE VI

PORTRAIT OF JAMES II, AS DUKE OF YORK. AFTER TENIERS. P, 1424.

PLATE VII

Ciuis Londinenſis Filia.

CIVIS Londinenſis Vxor.

Ciuis Londinenſis melioris qualitatis Vxor.

TITLE AND THREE PLATES FROM THE *THEATRUM MULIERUM* (AULA VENERIS). P. 1805, 1895, 1894, 1893.

PLATE VIII

The cold, not cruelty makes her weare **Winter** For a smoother skinn at night
In Winter, furrs and Wild beasts haire Embraceth her with more delight.

WINTER, WITH CORNHILL IN THE BACKGROUND. 30.

PLATE IX

THE THAMES AT WESTMINSTER, SEEN FROM THE QUAY AT LAMBETH HOUSE.
FROM AN ORIGINAL DRAWING IN PEN AND INK IN THE BRITISH MUSEUM.

THE TOWER OF LONDON. FROM AN ORIGINAL DRAWING IN PEN AND INK AND WATER-COLOUR IN THE BRITISH MUSEUM

PLATE X

WESTMINSTER ABBEY. FROM AN ORIGINAL DRAWING IN PEN AND INK IN THE
PEPYS LIBRARY, MAGDALENE COLLEGE, CAMBRIDGE.

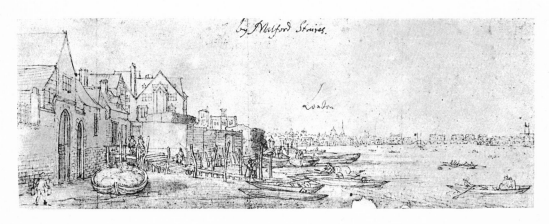

LONDON BY MILFORD STAIRES. FROM AN ORIGINAL DRAWING IN PEN AND INK IN THE PEPYS LIBRARY.
A STUDY FOR THE ETCHING, No. 80.

PLATE XI

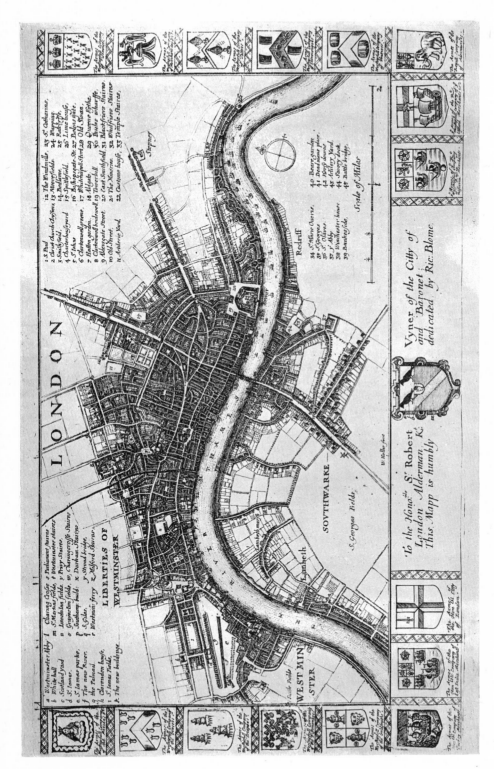

BIRD'S-EYE PLAN OF LONDON BEFORE THE FIRE. 8.

PLATE XII

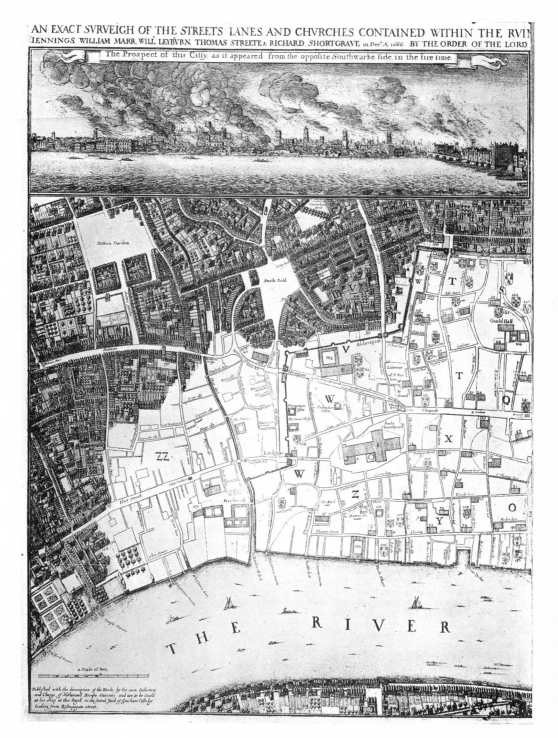

PLATE XIII

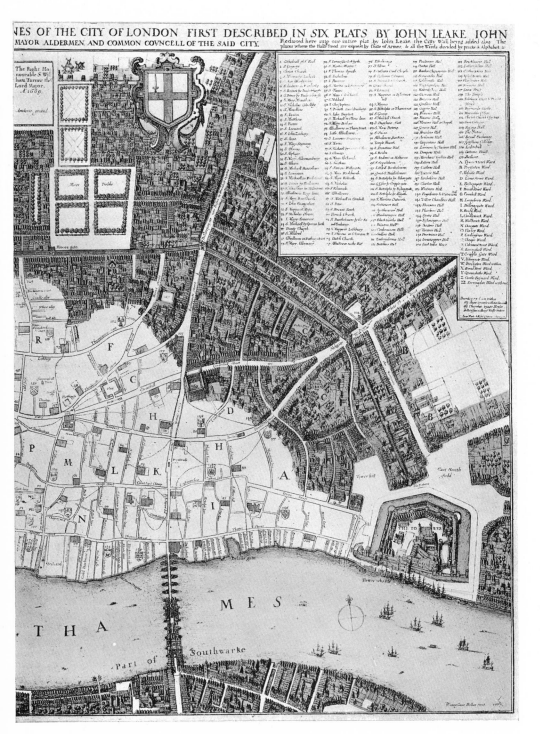

NES OF THE CITY OF LONDON FIRST DESCRIBED IN SIX PLATS BY IOHN LEAKE IOHN

MAYOR ALDERMEN AND COMMON COVNCELL OF THE SAID CITY.

WITHIN THE RUINS OF THE CITY OF LONDON (1669). 12.

PLATE XIV

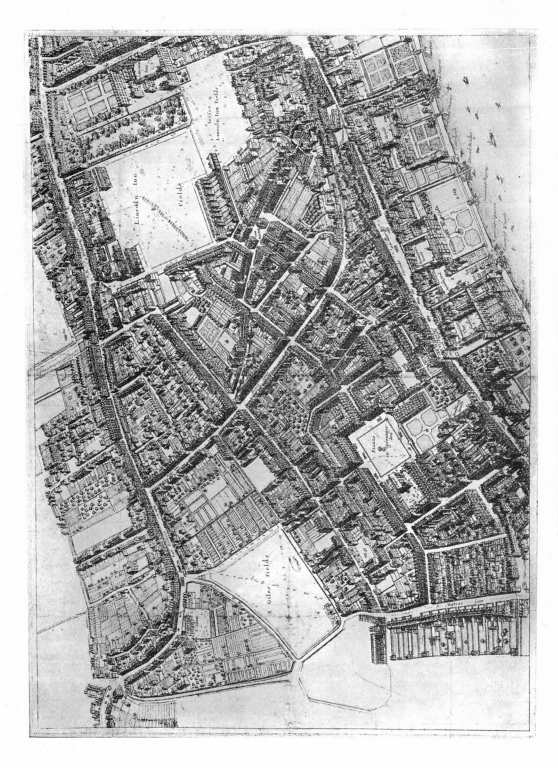

PLATE XV

LONG BIRD'S-EYE VIEW OF LONDON FROM BANKSIDE (1647). 16.

THE LEFT END-PIECE.

THE RIGHT END-PIECE.

PLATE XVI

LONDON FROM BANKSIDE, CONTINUED.

PLATE XVII

LONDON FROM BANKSIDE, CONTINUED.

PLATE XVIII

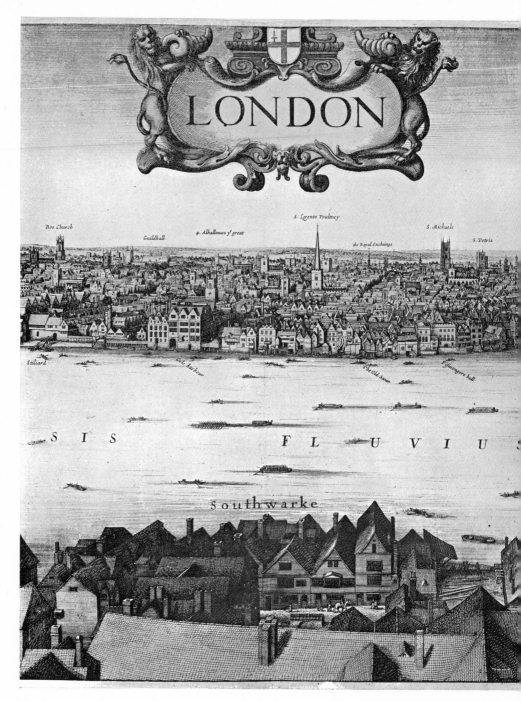

LONDON FROM BANKSIDE, CONTINUED.

PLATE XIX

LONDON FROM BANKSIDE, CONTINUED.

PLATE XX

The Tower.

Tower Wharfe

S. Olafe

LONDON FROM BANKSIDE, CONTINUED.

London from Bankside, 1647

{Plate XXa}

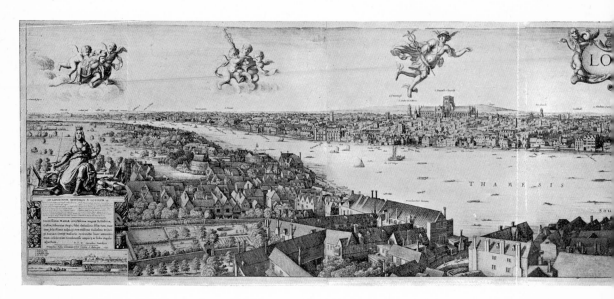

A SMALLER REPRODUCTION OF LONDON FROM BANKSIDE, JOINED UP IN ONE PIECE (1647). 16.

PLATE XXI

THE LONDINOPOLIS VIEW OF LONDON. 17

PLATE XXII

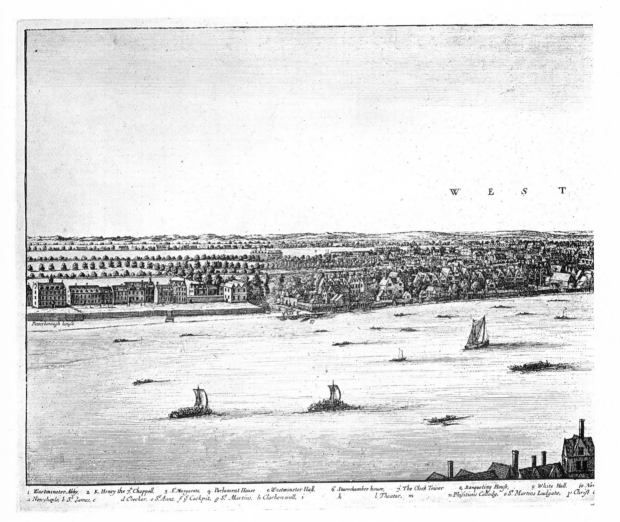

WEST

Petterborough house

1. Westminster Abby, 2. K. Henry the 7 Chappoll, 3. S: Margarets, 4. Parlament House v. Westminster Hall, 6 Starrchamber house, 7. The Clock Tower 8. Banqueting House, 9 White Hall. 10 Nor
a Newchaple, b S: James, c d Checker, e S: Anns, f S: Cockpit, g S: Martins, h Clarkenwell, i k l Theator, m n Phistions Colledg, o S: Martins Ludgate, p Christ

THE PROSPECT OF LONDON AND WESTMINSTER TAKEN FROM LAMBETH. 18. LEFT END.

PLATE XXIII

Taken from Lan

THE PROS
LON
WESTM

MINSTER

LAMBETH

umberland House, 11. Yorke House, 12. Durham yard, G. 14. 15 The Savoy, 16. Somerset House 17. 18 Essex House, 19. S. Clemens 20 The Temple.
urch, q S. Andrews Wardrobe, r S. Bennets Pauls wharfe, s S. Austins, t S. Martin Oldfishstreet, u S. Nichs: Cole: abby, w S. Mary Sommerset, x S. Mild: ll Bredstreet, y S. Laurence, z Quene Hith

PLATE XXIV

TAKEN FROM LAMBETH, CONTINUED. 18.

PLATE XXV

D O N

eral. 31 S Dunstans East 32 The Tower, 33 S'Marie Overies. 34 S' Olauer, 35 S' Georges. 36 Beare house, 37. The Ferry. 38. Parlament staires 39 Westminster bridge 40 Whitehall
at Grace church. at S' Dunes Backchurch, at Monument, an ao ax Alhallowes Barking, ay 42 Armoury in y Tower. Staires

SHEET 4

THE PROSPECT OF LONDON AND WESTMINSTER TAKEN FROM LAMBETH. 18. RIGHT END,

Parallel Views of London Before and After the Fire

{Plates XXVI-XXVII}

PLATE XXVI

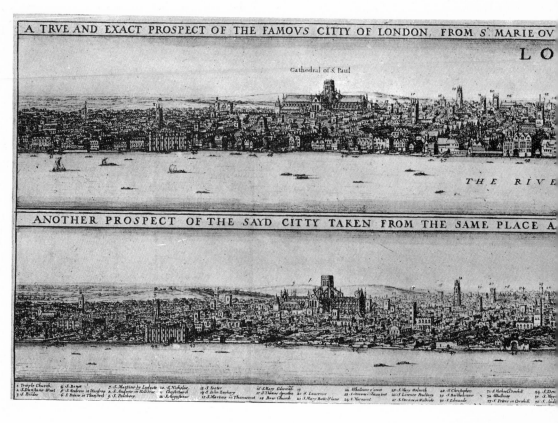

PLATE XXVII

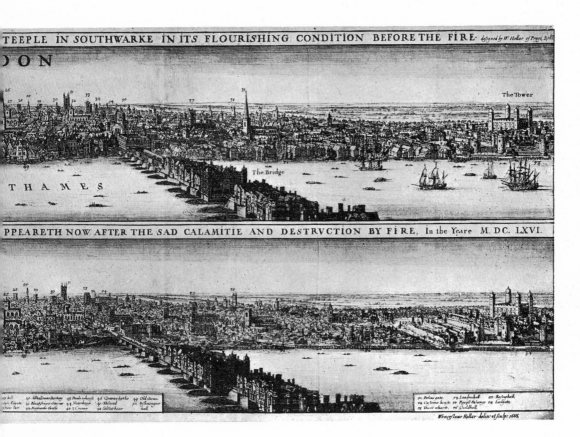

TEEPLE IN SOUTHWARKE IN ITS FLOURISHING CONDITION BEFORE THE FIRE. *designed by W. Hollar of Prage, Bohe*

OON

THAMES

The Tower

The Bridge

PPEARETH NOW AFTER THE SAD CALAMITIE AND DESTRVCTION BY FIRE, In the Yeare M. DC. LXVI.

Wenceslaus Hollar delin: et sculp: 1666

BEFORE AND AFTER THE FIRE. 19.

PLATE XXVIII

GREENWICH. 20. LEFT END.

PLATE XXIX

GREENWICH. 20 RIGHT END.

PLATE XXX

ST. MARY OVERY'S (ST. SAVIOUR'S, SOUTHWARK). 26.

ST. KATHERINE'S BY THE TOWER. 21.

PLATE XXXI

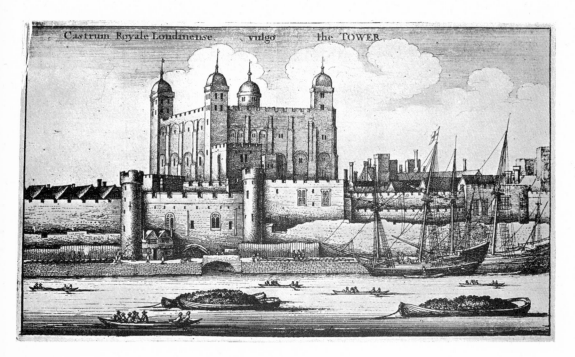

THE TOWER. 22.

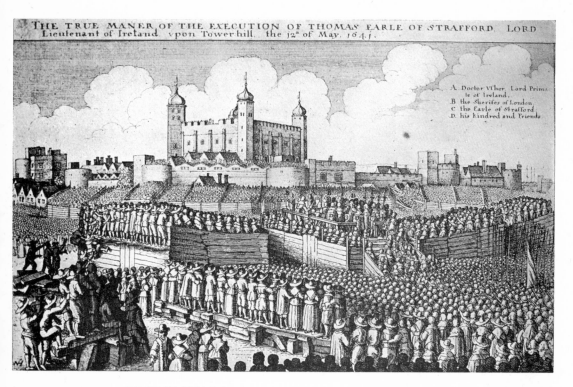

THE TOWER, WITH THE EXECUTION OF THE EARL OF STRAFFORD. 23.

PLATE XXXII

THE ROYAL EXCHANGE. INTERIOR, FACING SOUTH. 28.

PLATE XXXIII

The 2 of May. 1643. y⁰ Croſſe in Cheapeſide was pulled downe, a Troope of Horſe & 2 Companies of foote wayted to garde it & at y⁰ fall of y⁰ tope Croſſe dromes beat trupets blew & multitudes of Capes warre throwne in y⁰ Ayre, & a greate [...] of the Croſſe, & 6 day y⁰ 2 of May the Almana Popes burnt, in the pla ringinge of Bells, & a no hurt done in all — Shoute of People with ioy, ke ſareth, was y⁰ invention at night was the Leaden ce where it ſtood with greate Acclamation & theſe actions.

10 of May the Boocke of Sportes vpon the Lords day was burnt by the Hangman in the place where the Croſſe ſtoode, & at Exhange.

THE DESTRUCTION OF THE CROSS IN CHEAPSIDE. 31.

PLATE XXXIV

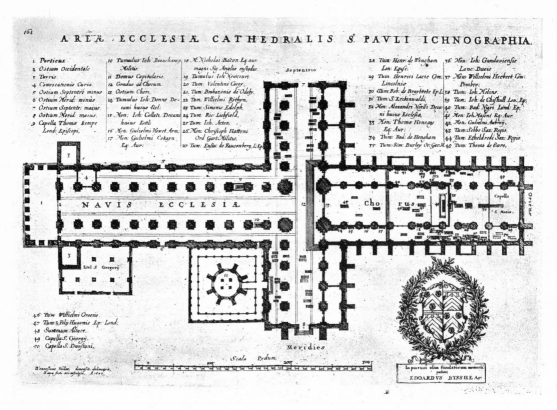

GROUND PLAN OF OLD ST. PAUL'S. 36.

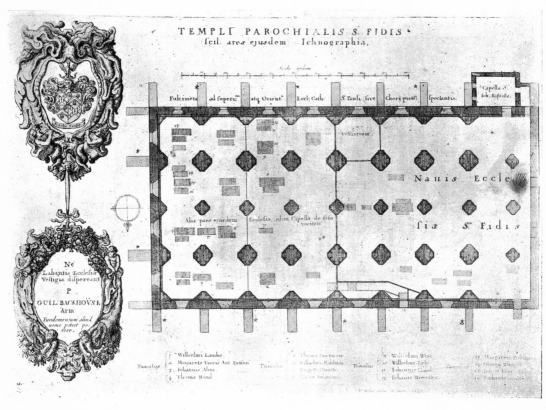

OLD ST. PAUL'S, GROUND PLAN OF THE CRYPT. 82.

PLATE XXXV

SOUTH VIEW OF OLD ST. PAUL'S, WITH THE SPIRE. 35.

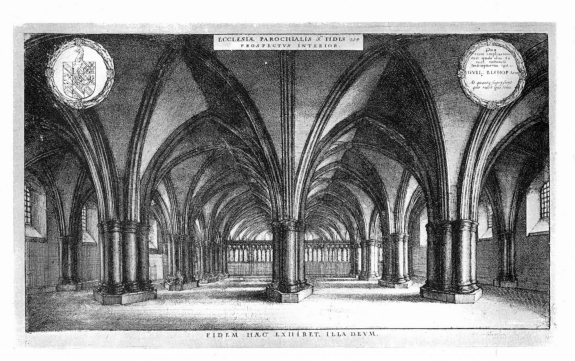

OLD ST. PAUL'S   VIEW OF THE CRYPT. 33.

PLATE XXXVI

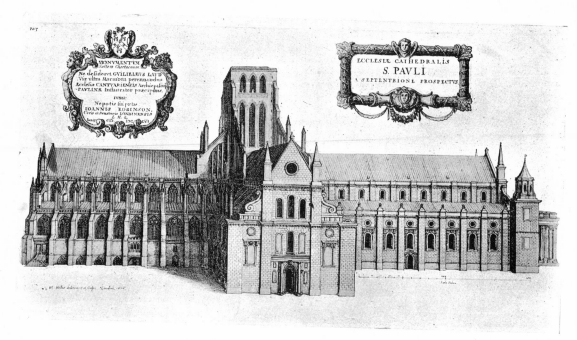

OLD ST. PAUL'S. EXTERIOR. NORTH. 38.

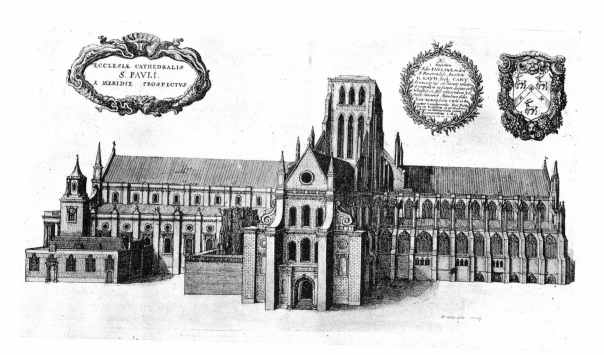

OLD ST. PAUL'S. EXTERIOR. SOUTH. 37.

PLATE XXXVII

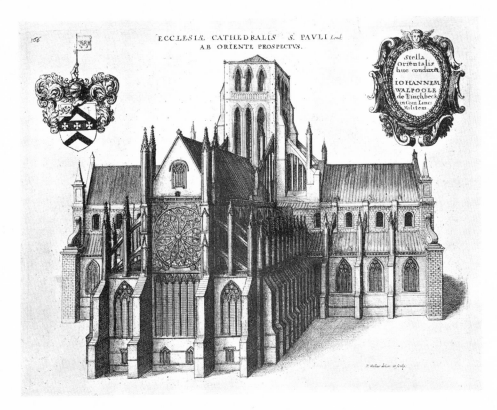

OLD ST. PAUL'S. EXTERIOR. EAST. 41.

OLD ST. PAUL'S. EXTERIOR. WEST. 39.

PLATE XXXVIII

OLD ST. PAUL'S. THE CHAPTER HOUSE. 34.

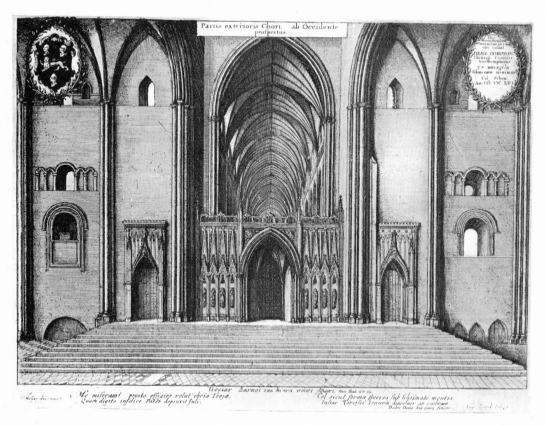

OLD ST. PAUL'S. INTERIOR: THE EXTERIOR OF THE CHOIR FROM THE WEST. 44.

PLATE XXXIX

NAVIS ECCLESIÆ CATHEDRALIS   S. PAVLI.
PROSPECTVS   INTERIOR.

Sit rediviva mater Ecclesia et pereant Sacrilegi ut navis Ecclesiæ temporum fluctibus immersura, salutaribus Dei auspiciis conservetur Majorum pietatem imitando mirentur posteri ut stupenda hæc Basilica antiquitus fundata et jamjam collapsura, tanquam sacrum Religionis Christianæ Monumentum in æternum sufflaminetur,

OLD ST. PAUL'S, INTERIOR, THE NAVE. 42.

PLATE XL

CHORI ECCLESIÆ CATHEDRALIS S. PAVLI PROSPECTVS INTERIOR.

Ne facra Dei ædis, au
guftiung adis PAVLINÆ
facrarium (longa tempo-
ris injuria, et facrilegâ fe-
quutoris faeculi incuriâ rui
turum) vel finifer labora
ret Annalium fides. ingen
tem hunc CHORVM, reli
gione ingenti facrum in
iconifmo fuperftitem
else voluit.
ELIAS ASHMOLE
ARMIGER.

OLD ST. PAUL'S. INTERIOR : THE CHOIR, FACING EAST. 45.

PLATE XLI

170

GUIL WALTER
primogenitus Guil
Walter de Saresden
in agro Oxon:
Baronetti
P.

Ecclesiæ Paulinæ moles sacra
Pietatis avitæ documentum,
Semo. et sacrilego ruitura
Sequioris seculi opprobrium
Tantum Religio potuit

'ORIENTALIS PARTIS ECCL. CATH. S. PAVLI, PROSPECTVS INTERIOR.

OLD ST. PAUL'S. INTERIOR: THE EAST END. 46.

PLATE XLII

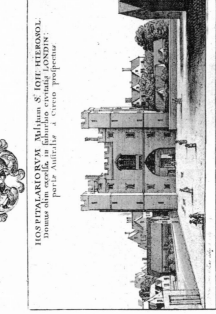

THE PRIORY OF ST. JOHN OF JERUSALEM. 70.

PLATE XLIII

THE WATERHOUSE BY ISLINGTON. 76.

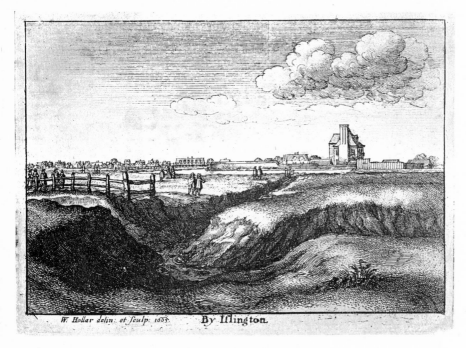

BY ISLINGTON (WITH THE WATERHOUSE). 74.

PLATE XLIV

BY THE WATERHOUSE. 72.

YE WATERHOUSE. 77.

PLATE XLV

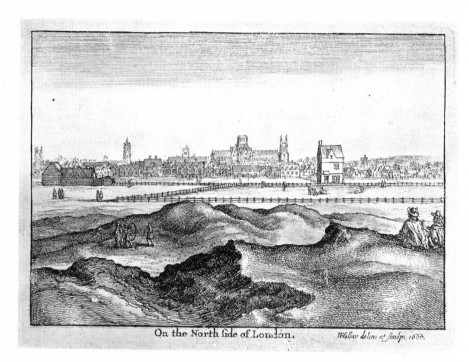

ON THE NORTH SIDE OF LONDON (WITH OLD ST. PAUL'S IN THE DISTANCE). 75.

BY ISLINGTON (WITH OLD ST. PAUL'S IN THE DISTANCE). 73.

PLATE XLVI

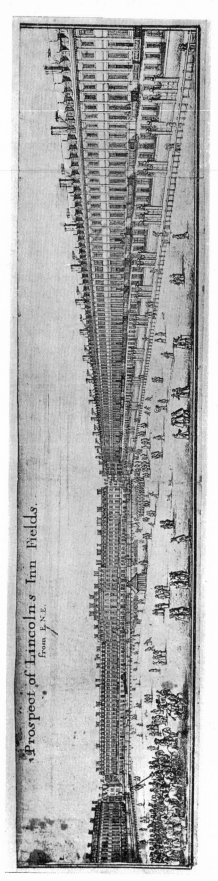

Prospect of Lincolns Inn Fields.
from E.N.E.

LINCOLN'S INN FIELDS. 78.

PLATE XLVII

PIAZZA in Coventgarden.

THE PIAZZA IN COVENT GARDEN. 79.

PLATE XLVIII

LONDON FROM THE TOP OF ARUNDEL HOUSE. 81.

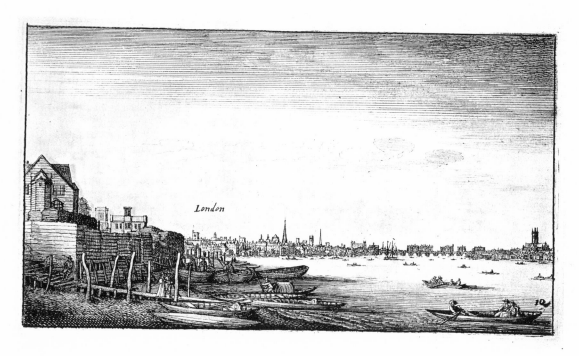

LONDON BY MILFORD STAIRES. 80.

PLATE XLIX

THE SAVOY. 84.

THE COURTYARD OF ARUNDEL HOUSE: THE SOUTH SIDE. 82.

THE COURTYARD OF ARUNDEL HOUSE: THE NORTH SIDE. 83.

PLATE L

WHITEHALL FROM THE RIVER. 85.

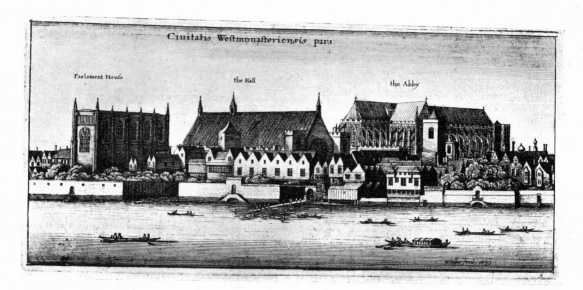

PART OF WESTMINSTER, WITH PARLIAMENT HOUSE, WESTMINSTER HALL, AND THE ABBEY, FROM THE RIVER. 86.

PLATE LI

NEW PALACE YARD, WITH WESTMINSTER HALL, AND THE CLOCK HOUSE. 90.

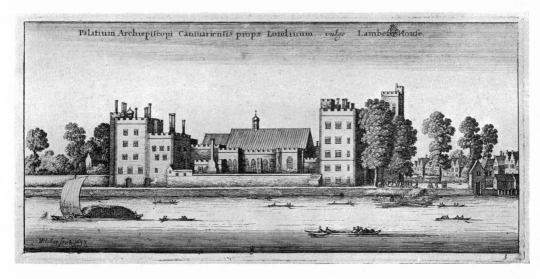

LAMBETH PALACE. 107.

PLATE LII

THE TRIAL OF ARCHBISHOP LAUD IN THE HOUSE OF LORDS. 88.

PLATE LIII

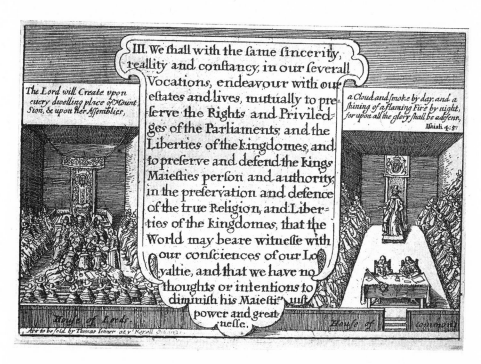

THE HOUSES OF LORDS AND COMMONS DURING SITTINGS. 89.

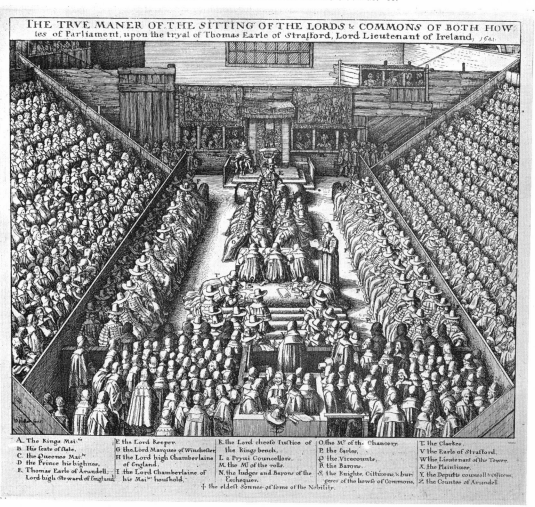

WESTMINSTER HALL. INTERIOR, WITH THE TRIAL OF THE EARL OF STRAFFORD. 91

PLATE LIV

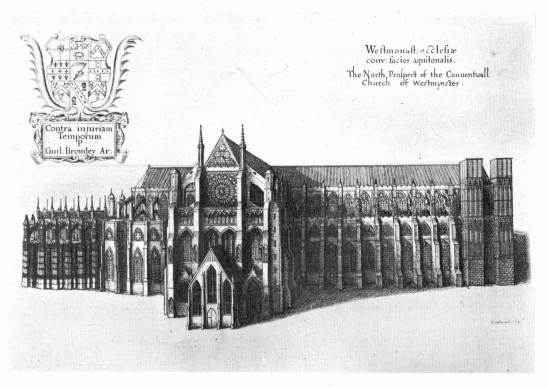

Westmonaſt: eccleſiæ
conv: facies aquilonalis.

The North Proſpect of the Conuentuall
Church of Weſtmynſter.

Contra injuriam
Temporum
P
Guil: Bromley Ar:

WESTMINSTER ABBEY. EXTERIOR: NORTH. 99.

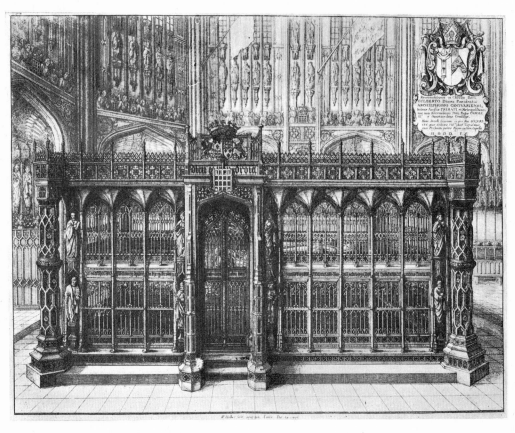

WESTMINSTER ABBEY. THE TOMB OF HENRY VII. 102.

PLATE LV

WESTMINSTER ABBEY. EXTERIOR: WEST. 100.

PLATE LVI

THE CORONATION OF CHARLES II IN WESTMINSTER ABBEY.   101

PLATE LVII

WHITEHALL FROM THE RIVER, WITH LAMBETH IN THE DISTANCE. 98.

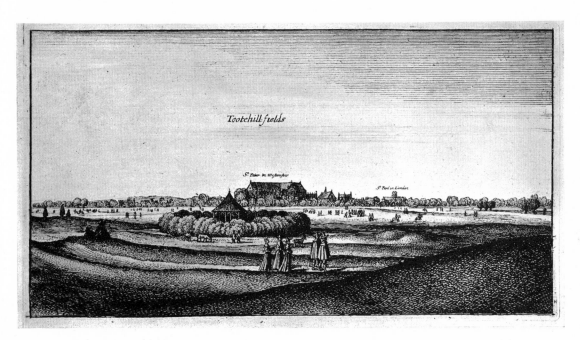

TOTHILL FIELDS. 106.

PLATE LVIII

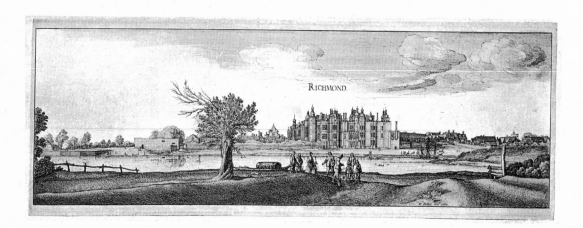

RICHMOND. 109.

WINDSOR CASTLE, FROM THE SOUTH, FROM A MAP OF BERKSHIRE. 112.

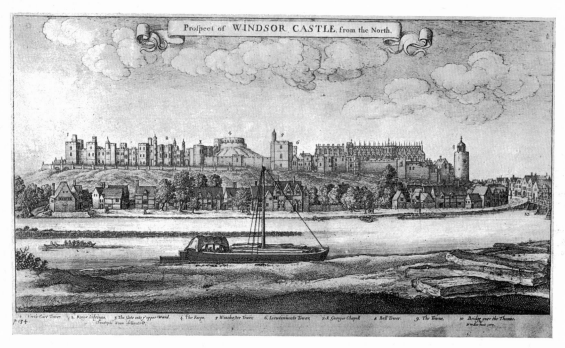

WINDSOR CASTLE, FROM THE NORTH. 116.

PLATE LIX

WINDSOR CASTLE, FROM THE SOUTH-EAST. 113.

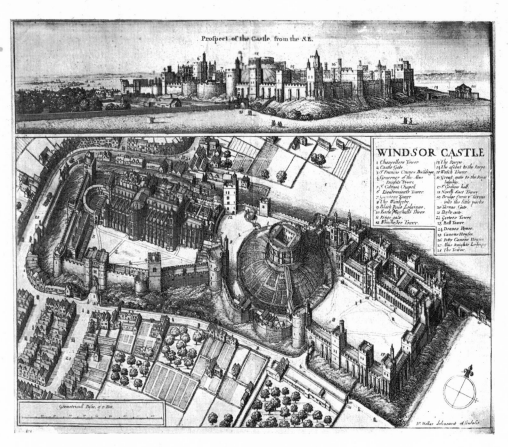

WINDSOR CASTLE. TWO VIEWS, ONE ABOVE THE OTHER. 114.

PLATE LX

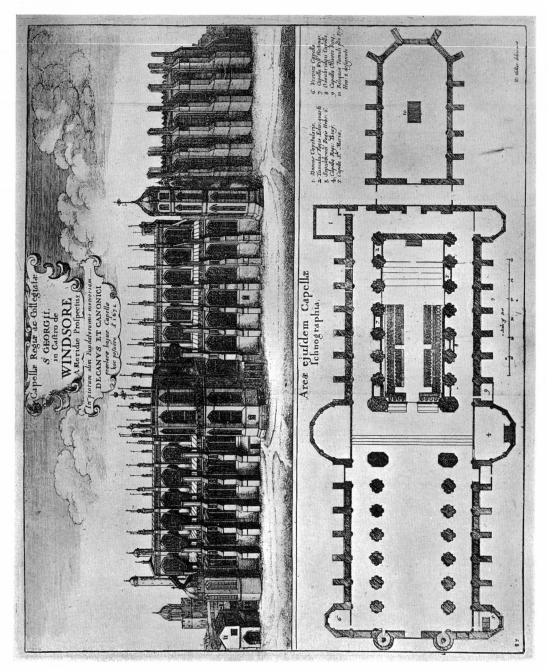

ST. GEORGE'S CHAPEL, WINDSOR CASTLE. EXTERIOR FROM THE SOUTH, AND GROUND PLAN. 119.

PLATE LXI

ST. GEORGE'S CHAPEL, WINDSOR CASTLE. INTERIOR: THE NAVE. 121.

PLATE LXII

ST. GEORGE'S CHAPEL, WINDSOR CASTLE. INTERIOR: THE CHOIR, FROM THE WEST, 125.

PLATE LXIII

ETON COLLEGE CHAPEL. EXTERIOR, THE NORTH. 132.

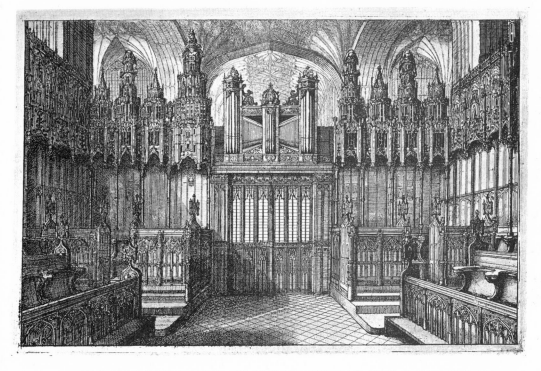

ST. GEORGE'S CHAPEL, WINDSOR CASTLE. THE CHOIR, WITH SCREEN AND ORGAN, FROM THE EAST. 124.

PLATE LXIV

A STATE BANQUET IN ST. GEORGE'S HALL, WINDSOR CASTLE. 131.